MW00435801

Lessons on Leadership (LOL)

For leaders who don't think
they need lessons on leadership

By Jim Ware,

Foreword by Michael Mezei,
President, Mawer Investment Management

9/2018

Tom —
Good leadership brings
out the best in people.
Here's hoping these ideas
help,
J Ware

© 2018 Focus Consulting Group

All rights reserved. No part of this book may be reproduced in any form without written permission of the copyright owner. Every effort has been made to ensure that credits accurately comply with information supplied. Because of the dynamic nature of the Internet, any web addresses or links contained in this book may have changed since publication and may no longer be valid.

CreateSpace Independent Publishing Platform

Additional praise for Lessons on Leadership

I have been reading Jim's work since his seminal work, Investment Leadership, hit the bookstand more than 10 years ago. Jim's research has influenced me and my firm deeply. This new book includes new research and more practical tips on achieving higher performance through shifting various dimensions of the organizational culture. We have become a better and happier organization from incorporating Jim's advice, which goes to prove, with a click on Amazon, you can buy happiness!

– Jason Hsu
Founder and Chief Investment Officer, Rayliant Global Advisors

I have worked with FCG for a number of years across different teams in our global business – in Europe, Asia and Africa. The insights of the FCG team are always valuable, bringing the best of global practice to bear on the specifics of our investment teams with focused and practical advice on improving team performance and hence client outcomes. I don't often believe that consultants bring wisdom, but it is true for FCG.

– Graham Mason
CIO, M&G Investments

Jim has a unique grasp of leadership within the investment management industry. Jim's abundance of experience combined with his efforts to continuously improve the industry make him the go-to person for many executives. Jim's writings provide nutrition to the culture of our firm (or any firm) and will fill the appetite of those seeking leadership knowledge.

– Stan C. Moss, CFA, CPA
Chief Executive Officer, Polen Capital Management

Jim and his team help leaders in the investment industry become level five leaders. Focus Consulting empowers firms to change from good to great by building a strong culture.

– Jayman Yi
Co-founder & PM, Roehl & Yi Investment Advisors, LLC

"In my 40+ years as a portfolio manager I have come across only a handful of original thinkers. You see, original thinkers do not think outside the box; they don't even care if there is a box. Jim Ware is an original thinker. I have read every book he has ever written. You should too."

Fred Martin
Founder and former CEO,
Disciplined Growth Investors

I've had the pleasure and privilege of working with Jim Ware CFA (and his colleagues at FCG) for over 14 years….with two different institutions (both public and private). I can honestly say that I consider Jim one of my most trusted sources of insight, cultural learnings and personal coaching. Jim is the rarest of all talents in that he deeply understands our business and the wealth management / investment industry, but more importantly…..he has a unique perspective on people, talent and culture that I have found invaluable during my career. My colleagues and I have worked hard to build our team and our culture around Jim's thoughtful work. In short, Jim (and FCG) is a gift to our industry and those who have a leadership role in the business."

– Stephen R. Mullin
Managing Director, Private Client Group, Fort Washington Investments

"Jim Ware takes you through the crucial skills that all leaders need to work on. Ware has a good writing style that simplifies the complexities that leaders face, such as accountability, culture building, teamwork and so on. The book challenges leaders to continually improve. I plan to give it to my leadership team. It's the kind of book you read, then later re-read. Highly recommend it."

George Mavroudis
President & Chief Executive Officer,
Guardian Capital Group Limited

Acknowledgments

For this book, I especially want to thank all our clients, whose leaders have opened themselves up to the leadership journey. This step takes courage, curiosity, and an openness to self-awareness. These leaders have taken a big step towards conscious leadership. If all leaders were willing to take this step, the world would be a better place. I know, bold statement, but I completely believe it. When leaders improve, everyone wins.

I also thank my team mates – Keith, Liz, Michael, Jamie, Bryan, and Laura – who have inspired me, supported me, coached me, and loved me. Yes, loved me. The more I learn about leadership and strong culture, the more I believe that the "L" word is core to success. In the case of my team mates, we care deeply about one another and offer feedback on a regular basis: critical or appreciative. Hence, we improve. (Team mates, if you are withholding from me, now would be a good time to tell me…)

I have many teachers, counselors, coaches, and friends who provide valuable insights. I thank them greatly for their help and wisdom. They include: Carol Saunders, Greg and Lynn Barrette, David Ellzey, Richard Barrett, Hale Dwoskin, Paul Zavagno, David Daniels, Helen Palmer, Jerry Wagner, Eckhart Tolle, Buddha, and a host of others. Oh yes, and Jesus as well.

Finally, I thank my "base camp" members who provide love and support as I make my way up the mountain. Janey, my wife and life partner of 20 years. Our two beautiful children, Alex and Nikki. Our three dogs – Kobe, Teton, and Lola – who demonstrate unconditional love. Many readers will have heard me talk about my Mother-in-Law, Marilyn, who is perhaps my greatest teacher of all.

The older I get, the more I appreciate the value of connection. Without all of these connections, I couldn't even begin to contribute meaningfully. I am blessed to love what I do. I sincerely hope that it helps make the world a better place.

Lessons on Leadership (LOL):

For leaders who don't think they need lessons on leadership

Jim Ware

Foreword

I first heard Jim Ware's name during the spring of 2008 when interviewing for the role as President of Mawer Investment Management Ltd. (an independent investment manager in Calgary, Alberta). The interview process included an assessment by some guy named Jim Ware at Focus Consulting Group (FCG), a Chicago-based firm that had helped Mawer with strategy and culture for over 10 years. Although I didn't know what to expect, Jim and I had a delightful conversation about my motivation to work in the investment industry, culture, managing teams, and my leadership approach and journey. At that time, I had no idea this would be the first of many interactions with Jim and his colleagues at FCG over the next 10 years. Or that they would play a large role not only in shaping Mawer's culture, but my leadership journey at the firm.

Culture came up repeatedly during the many interviews, and although I got the job I didn't really get the importance of culture. I had been schooled in "what gets measured gets done", hard-nosed, bottom-line oriented business environments, where values were seen as nice words on a website and culture a 'soft' HR type of thing. I was given *High Performance Investment Teams* (Wiley, 2008) as a must read and started hearing language like "staying above the line", "holding that lightly" and avoiding "sludge". At firm-wide and team workshops, I witnessed Jim's talent of conveying the importance of culture, while being interesting, even entertaining, and highly informative at the same time. I was starting to get it: we come together within firms because we think we can do a better job as investors, in meeting client expectations, in operating and managing risk, by working collectively in teams better than any one of us could possibly do on our own. Culture is the grease and values -- the glue that makes it all work. Jim often says that great culture leads to high workability: the ability to get things done quickly and with ease. Doing that right is hard, yet critical to success. That's been our experience at Mawer.

This book is about leadership and leadership journeys. Jim and Keith Robinson have played a large role in shaping mine. It's safe to say that I came into the President's role at Mawer believing what I now consider to be leadership myths. Things like: it's lonely at the top; you need to have all the answers; it's all about the bottom line; you need to be tough (nice guys finish last); and leadership is highly stressful leaving little time or energy for anything else.

Jim helped open my eyes to other possibilities, and gave me, and many and others at Mawer, the tools to reshape my leadership journey in a way that is authentic to who I am and who we are as a firm. It's not "lonely at the top" if you have a trusted group of colleagues and share responsibilities as a team. And you don't need to have all the answers if you retain your humility, stay open and curious to other perspectives, and establish clear decision rights. As a leader, you don't need to "be tough" but you do need to be able to make tough decisions (such as dealing with difficult people), speak candidly and give and remain open to feedback.

FCG has also helped me understand and embrace self-awareness as a starting place for knowing and helping others - tools like the Enneagram Personality Assessment have helped me understand that different styles and opinions are not right or wrong, they are just different. Understanding them leads to more productive discussions and decisions, while avoiding unnecessary conflict and drama.

Through Jim, I have realized that authentic, values-based servant leadership is not only OK, it is welcomed. Of course, results matter, for clients and the firm, but our work together has helped me understand the importance of culture and effective leadership in achieving them, while making the journey a whole lot more fun and satisfying.

As you read the pages that follow, whether you experience an 'aha moment' that helps you understand yourself or one of your colleagues better, gain an insight into what you need to start/stop doing as a leader, or just simply have a chuckle, I hope that you enjoy and find value in these insights as much as I have over the years.

– Michael Mezei, President, Mawer Investment Management

(Mawer is an independent, employee-owned, investment management firm based in Calgary, with offices in Toronto and Singapore, with 155 people and CDN $52 billion AUM for institutional and individual clients.)

Introduction

I'm sorry. Your boss probably set this book on your desk with a note: "Read this." And your predictable response was, "Oh, crap. Can't I read something by Taleb, Ellis, Buffett, or a classic by Benjamin Graham?" Most investment professionals (hereafter called just *pros*) would rather get a root canal without Novocaine. Understandable. Pros have a natural aversion to all the "soft" stuff like leadership. Some have expressed their frustration as simply: "Why can't people just get their work done!? Why do we need to hold their hands? Or be nice to them? Hey, grow up! Get the job done!"

All well and good, but as one wag put it, "In theory everything should work, in practice it doesn't." It would be nice if we were all Mr. Spock (*Star Trek* Vulcan) who was purely rational—but we're not. Especially the pros who *say* they are (and then get pissed off when you challenge them and yell at you). We are all emotional and flawed and need some guidance in managing ourselves. Good leaders understand this reality and have developed skills to bring out the best in individuals and teams.

The investment world is woefully short of good leaders. Don't get me wrong, the pros with whom I've worked over decades are bright, engaging, often funny, very decent folks. No question. But they have big blindspots concerning the importance of collaboration. Interestingly, one of the most common values of investment firms is precisely that: teamwork and collaboration. A great deal of lip service is paid to the soft stuff but very few resources are devoted to skill development. One quick example: At a conference, I asked CFOs in a live poll, "Where does culture fit in your budgeting plans:

1. Top priority?
2. Secondary priority?
3. Or not on the radar screen?"

Fifty-five percent of the CFOs responded with the third choice. Another factoid culled from hundreds of investment firms surveyed: the largest gap between what firms *have* in their culture versus what the staff *wants* is leadership development/mentoring. See what I mean about the blindspot? The biggest "ask" in the investment world is the subject explored in this book: *How do we develop leaders?*

My guess at the explanation for this blindspot is the history of the industry. Up until recently, the industry was so profitable that monkeys could manage the firm and it would still be successful. Why? Because a handful of skilled investors working with a good distribution team could produce results without much oversight. Pros love this work and don't need a leader to push them. Further, regulation was modest enough that large compliance efforts weren't necessary. Information technology (IT) demands were such that exploring artificial intelligence (AI) and developing world-class data resources weren't crucial to success. Finally, the profit margins weren't being squeezed, so planning, budgeting, and execution weren't essential. (In fact, many smaller boutique firms didn't even have budgets!)

But all that has changed. Investment firms really have to be well led these days. Leaders must bring out the best in their people. They must build excellent cultures that attract, develop, and retain top talent. Executive committees (ECs) must collaborate well and demonstrate the behaviors of top teams. Talent reviews, performance assessments, ongoing feedback, succession plans, fair compensation, and a host of other factors play heavily into success.

By the way, for the purpose of defining our terms, the preceding paragraph is a good working definition of *leadership*. More on that in Chapter 2.

When I first started as an analyst in 1980, with Gary Brinson as my boss, my job was to analyze industries and stay out of trouble. (Which I largely managed to do, except when I bought more than 5% of Scott Foresman stock. Gary found out and approached my desk at high speed, shouting, "Do you want to put me in prison?" After that little encounter, I was told by the seasoned members, "Well, you're officially a team member now …") We didn't have elaborate management systems. We operated from an apprenticeship model. My immediate boss, Bob Moore, was a lovely guy who taught me how to analyze companies. Brinson was an incredibly astute investment strategist who crafted a vision of success well beyond the then-current state of the industry. And so Brinson Partners succeeded beautifully because of innate wisdom and clear strategy. In my view, those days are gone. Wisdom and strategy are still essential, but now much more is required.

Hence the need for a book like this. And again, I'm sorry. I know you are reading this under protest. But in your heart of hearts, you know I'm right. Now investment success depends on more skillful leadership and followership. I'm not sure three smart people and a Bloomberg will succeed in today's environment, and they certainly will stumble if they scale up to become a sizeable firm.

So, the bad news is you have to read this book. But the good news is that I will try to make it both enjoyable and valuable—and if you take it to heart, *it will help*. You will improve your leadership of self, team, and firm.

I've been writing short pieces—Lessons on Leadership (LOLs)—for years, trying to capture insights and share them with industry pros. If you have been faithfully reading those writings, you will have a good idea of the lessons that follow here.

This book is designed to allow readers to pick and choose topics that interest them. Of course, you can read it straight through. I've written it in what I hope is a friendly style, allowing easy access to useful tips. The logic of the chapters is as follows:

1. Purpose: why our work matters
I start with purpose because industry participants—both young and older—are awakening to a question: *why* am I doing this work? What is important about the investment profession? How does this work contribute to a better world? As will be discussed in Chapter 1, 70% of the industry participants feel passion for their work,[1] but only 17% found it meaningful. That's changing. The millennials are much more purpose-driven. To attract and retain new talent, leaders will have to connect the dots for millennials and explain convincingly that investments play a critical role in people's well-being, which of course it does. Chapter 1 elaborates on the topic of purpose, with data and stories to help leaders see and act on it.

2. Leadership: a necessary nuisance
Jumping into the main topic, Chapter 2 reviews Focus Consulting Group's (FCG's) research, consulting, and coaching experience with hundreds of investment leaders. What are the leaders' strengths? Their weaknesses? Blindspots? What steps are involved in improving their leadership?

3. Culture: who are we as a firm? What do we stand for?
A major task for leaders is developing good culture; FCG is probably best known for its culture work. In this chapter I share what we've learned about creating the proper mindset to execute on the strategy. Despite all the lip service paid to strong culture, most firms still don't elevate it to a top priority, as you read earlier relating to the CFO polling—and these are the same firms that undoubtedly tout their culture as "excellent" in the finals presentations! I'll provide insights about how the best firms actually invest in and build high-performance cultures.

4. Trust: the platform for performance
Trust could arguably be the first and most important chapter in this book. Without strong trust, firms flounder. The three most important elements of strong culture are purpose, trust, and values. FCG does many assignments involving trust with executive committees (ECs) and teams throughout an organization. Many times, we discover that trust is remarkably low in a firm. The main reason is that raising trust issues is, well, awkward.

It's hard to say to a co-worker: "I don't trust you and here's why." That won't be a pleasant conversation. Nevertheless, top teams that understand the importance of trust know how to address these issues, resolve them, and move on, allowing for much more effectiveness and efficiency.

5. Teams: where the work gets done

Teams are the basic unit of any organization. That's where the work gets done … and given weak interpersonal skills, many investment teams suffer. In this chapter, I unpack what it means to be a *team* and how the best ones operate. Part of being a good team is having stated ground rules for efficient collaboration. FCG has long practiced and taught the "core four" behaviors that lead to optimal performance. I describe those and include thoughts on conflict resolution. Conflict is inevitable in any family, team, or other group, so dealing with it is essential.

6. Difficult people: The red X

A phrase coined by FCG, the *Red X* is the person who creates drama on a team. Often, such people are a bad fit with a given culture: for example, a pro who likes to work independently joins a firm that is heavily oriented toward collaboration. But the Red X can also be a person who is difficult to work with in general: self-centered, sarcastic, condescending, and the like. These situations present a tough leadership challenge. Do you try to change the Red X through coaching? Do you hope that the situation will resolve itself over time? Do you put the Red Xs on probation? Or just fire them immediately?

7. Accountability: defining it and executing on it

Accountability is absolutely essential for strong culture, and the most requested skill that FCG is asked to address. When firms discover that they need to reduce the bad behaviors in their culture—gossip, blame, politics, defensiveness, and the like—they choose accountability as the antidote. And with good reason. There is much evidence to suggest that accountability, if deployed and done correctly, can improve the efficiency and effectiveness of a firm's operations. (By the way, accountability does *not* mean "find out who screwed up and blame them as quickly as possible.")

8. Emotional intelligence (EQ): becoming people smart

The lowest score for investment pros on 360 assessments is *emotional intelligence* (EQ). This term lumps together several interpersonal skills—self-awareness, awareness of others, and self-management—and culminates in the overall ability to collaborate well with others. Given that many investment pros are individual contributors by nature—good at doing their own work, independent of others—their EQ skills are often undeveloped. This chapter describes the skills and provides tips on improving your own.

In addition to these topics, I've included some short essays on various topics that also seem useful for investment leaders, such as:

- Integrity: defining it beyond "do the right thing"
- Managing millennials: yes, they are different
- Strategy: can you say what yours is?
- Sales: it's a brave new world
- Feedback: learning to love it
- Givers and takers: savvy givers win out
- Complexity thinking: managing polarities
- Debates: making them open and productive
- Client-centric … really?

Though not exhaustive, these ideas—if understood and practiced—will put you way ahead of most investment pros. Obviously, you must continue to hone your technical skills, but research clearly shows that technical skills will only get you so far. Beyond that, you must work well with others and, if called upon, know how to lead them. It is my sincere wish that the writings in this book will help you do just that.

---

1   Suzanne Duncan & CFA Institute, *Discovering Phi: Motivation as the Hidden Variable of Performance* (October 2016); http://www.statestreet.com/content/dam/statestreet/documents/Articles/CAR/CAR_Phi_Web_FINAL.pdf

CHAPTER 1

Purpose: Why Our Work Matters

Have you thought about why you do investment work? Many investment pros haven't. They enjoy the work.[2] They certainly enjoy the income. They know *what* they do, and they know *how* they do it—but they haven't really answered the core question of *why*.

FCG believes the investment industry is missing a huge opportunity by responding to this question of "why?" with a blank stare. Or fumbling about with, "We're trying to create alpha." (Alpha is a "what" answer, not a "why" answer. You create alpha, but why? Why does the world—or the client—need alpha? And why is it meaningful or gratifying to create it? And is there a deeper why to the whole pursuit of alpha?)

To be sure, the CFA Institute and other industry groups have stepped up with "client-first" programs. The intention here is good: Fiduciaries *should* put their clients' interests first. Unfortunately, these programs are mostly instituted in response to bad behavior and low Edelman Trust[3] scores for the industry. They don't really answer the "why?" question.

FCG has been investigating this purpose question (the "why?") for a long time now. It is becoming increasingly important as millennials[4] enter the workforce. They want to know: "Does our firm contribute to making a better world?" They are choosing purpose over profit. And while FCG acknowledges that both are important, we like their ordering: purpose, then profit.

At the other end of the age spectrum, baby boomers also are taking more interest in purpose. As Abraham Maslow, Ken Wilber, Richard Barrett, and others note in their research, there is a natural evolution from basic needs (safety, security, community, self-esteem) to higher wants: purpose, service, making a difference, and common good. Thus, both ends of the age continuum represented in the workforce seem to be searching for this deeper meaning: *why does our work matter?*

To give an example, my colleague Michael Falk and I were facilitating an investment offsite in which—to our surprise—the CIO started the second day with a video clip of Simon Sinek (author of *Start with Why*). Sinek argues that successful firms have a clear sense of mission. They understand the underlying "why?" of their business. After recovering from my initial shock—that a CIO would start the day with this clip—I asked him a predictable question, "So, what is *your* 'why?'" In a candid response, he said, "I've been thinking about it a lot. I'm not sure. I know what we do and how we do it, but I can't give you a clear reason for why." I share this story because it captures what we often experience in the industry: Good people, doing good work, but with no real answer to the "why?" question.

To continue the story, later at the offsite Michael Falk was asked to speak about his new book[5], commissioned by the CFA Research Institute, on sustainable economic growth and entitlement programs. Michael held up the book and said, "This is my 'why.' Ever since my twenties I've known that I want to positively influence the financial lives of as many people as possible." A powerful silence followed. The alignment and congruence were palpable. Michael loves investments. And he loves helping people. Michael's passion for his work is evident because it is purpose-driven.

If you're curious about your "why", you might try this exercise. Think of the three circles below and reflect on your answer for each:

Figure 1.1 Defining Individual Purpose

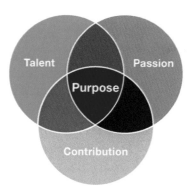

In Michael's case, would answer as follows:

- **Talent:** excellent analytical mind for researching and understanding complex subjects. Strong ability to communicate those insights to others.
- **Passion:** Using his talent to educate and help others
- **Contribution:** helping organizations and individuals make better financial choices

When you combine these three elements, you arrive at Michael's deep commitment to:

*I want to positively influence the financial
lives of as many people as possible.*

This experience set off a light bulb in my mind. Couldn't everyone in the investment world rally around this statement? Or a variation of it? I began to play with the statement and to bounce it off leaders in the investment world. The version I've landed on is:

*As a member of the investment profession, I commit
to positively influencing people's financial lives.*

Here's what I like about it. For starters, it's short and memorable—and it's very inclusive. When I bounced it off Britt Harris, CIO of UTIMCO, he immediately began exploring the possibilities:

- Helping people understand how to budget, save, and invest.
- Helping people understand the connection between healthy finances and good health.
- Helping with the whole topic of financial literacy.

Yes. All these activities could fit under this broad purpose statement. The statement works for active firms and passive firms. For institutional and retail. Regardless of your role in the investment firm, you could find a way that your efforts contribute to this mission. Some examples:

- **PM or financial analyst:** By researching and finding appropriate investments, the analyst contributes to the financial well-being of the client. By helping to allocate capital to successful firms, the analyst serves the economy.
- **Client service:** By understanding the client's needs and fashioning appropriate investment goals, the investment pro contributes to the client's financial well-being, and most likely peace of mind as well.
- **CIO:** By ensuring that a given firm's investment philosophy, process, and execution are sound, the CIO contributes to the overall goals, including the ones just mentioned.

I can imagine professionals in each of these roles, throughout the organization, embracing the broad purpose statement and then tying it to the work they are doing: trading, compliance, marketing, operations, and so on. Each person, asking herself or himself: "In my role, how do I positively influence people's financial lives?" We can tailor the general statement to our own passion and life purpose.

Moreover, FCG would encourage all investment professionals to expand their view of service from just their own clients to people at large. The broad purpose statement encourages investment professionals to move from a competitive (win/lose, zero-sum) mindset to a cooperative (win/win, abundance) mindset. Specifically, it allows us to say, "We support all people, everywhere, having financial well-being." Admittedly, that is a huge dream (think Martin Luther King, Jr.) but it is noble and inspirational—and each of us can do our small part in moving toward it. As with the Hippocratic Oath for medical doctors, the charge is to serve "all my fellow human beings"; not just my patients, or the rich ones, or the ones that I particularly like.[6] Imagine the change in our industry's reputation if investment professionals routinely stated that their mission was to **positively influence people's financial lives**. And meant it.

Personally, my deepest "why" would be to help people attain peace of mind about their finances. I know people who are multimillionaires but lose sleep over money.[7] That's crazy. So, my personal tie-in to the statement would be to help people realize that money won't buy happiness. The research is clear that above a certain level (around $75,000 per year, higher in major cities), money does not positively influence happiness. (If it did, all millionaires would be happy.) Happiness is an "inside" job. I'd like to help wealthy people realize that moving to the top of Maslow's hierarchy—purpose, service, common good—provides lasting joy. Money does not.

A quick story: An Eastern spiritual teacher was explaining his spiritual training to a Westerner. The final stage involved the monks meditating in the jungle amongst wild tigers. The Westerner exclaimed, "Oh, my! That is quite the test: to maintain your peace of mind with tigers prowling about!" The Eastern teacher replied, "Yes, in the East we have tigers. In the West, you have money." In many cases, money is dangerous to peace of mind. We've been trained to believe, "If I just had more money, I'd be happy." We can unlearn that to our betterment.

Back to the opening points in this chapter about millennials and boomers: Both age groups indicate a desire for a noble calling. And when we state our purpose as **positively influencing people's financial lives**, we are aligned with one.

In my view, Dan Pink gets it right when he says:

> Autonomous people working toward mastery perform at very high levels [e.g., most investment pros]. But those who do so in the service of some greater objective can achieve even more. The most deeply motivated people—not to mention those who are most productive and satisfied—hitch their desires to a cause larger than themselves.[8]

It's time for those in the "wealth" profession to realize that they are every bit as important as the "health" profession. People's basic needs include health and wealth. If either one is missing, the quality of life is severely and negatively affected. We may not be saving actual lives, but by saving financial lives, we have a huge impact on people's quality of life and pursuit of happiness.

So, where is the hard evidence that investment professionals are *not* operating from purpose? Table 1.1 shows FCG research on nearly one thousand investment pros.

Table 1.1 Motivation and Meaning

Motivation: What has the most meaning in daily experience?	
The work serves a larger purpose, doing something positive in the world (such as allocating capital property in the markets).	**8%**
The work contributes to a sound and sustainable financial future for our firm.	**15%**
The work benefits our clients, and I enjoy happy clients most of all about my job.	**23%**
The work allows me to spend time with bright and engaging colleagues. I like these team interactions best of all.	**22%**
The work is interesting, challenging, and intellectually stimulating.	**32%**

Note that only 8% of the pros state that they are motivated by a larger purpose. This number was similar in magnitude (i.e., small) to a study done by CFA Institute and State Street in which they showed that only about 17% of investment pros found purpose in their work.[9] Interestingly, though, some of the most successful firms that FCG works with show just the reverse of this result. They have established high purpose in their organizations. For example, Polen Capital is a very successful long-only equity boutique in Boca Raton, Florida. Its level of purpose was measured against the CFA/State Street norms with the results shown in Figure 1.2.

Figure 1.2 Polen Phi Score

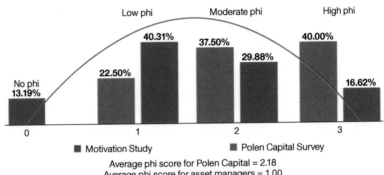

Average phi score for Polen Capital = 2.18
Average phi score for asset managers = 1.00

Source: State Street Center for Applied Research. Phiagnostic Survey, April 2017. Motivation Study, February 2016. Sample size: Polen Capital Survey = 40, Motivation Study = 1496

The "Phi" language in the CFA/State Street can be interpreted as "purpose driven." Increasingly, in FCG's work, we are seeing a correlation between strong purpose and good results. In Table 1.2, you see some of the older, more traditional mission statements contrasted with the newer, more motivational ones.

Table 1.2 Old Paradigms versus New, Purpose-Driven Paradigms

Old Paradigm	New Paradigm (in addition to investment return)
Grow our firm to $30 billion in 5 years. —ABC asset management	Our products, services, and investments should show both economic and social value for the future. —LGIM
Provide excellence in investing and client service. —XYZ investments	We are committed to transformative change for both our company and the communities in which we work. We donate 50% of our profits to non-profit organizations. —Bridgeway Capital Management
Have fun and make money. —Alpha management	You are here for a reason; We are here to support that. —Conscious Capital Wealth Management

With growing frequency, firms are asking FCG to consult on purpose statements. They ask, "How can we create a statement that honestly reflects the contribution we are making to our stakeholders: clients, employees, owners, and society?" The younger generation of workers is drawn to the firms that can connect the dots from the day-to-day work to the broader contribution to the world.

You might be thinking, "Okay, but can you give us a concrete example of how a CIO or Director of Research moves from the everyday life of an analyst to some greater purpose?" Marc Mayer provided an excellent one when he was Director of Research at Bernstein. He described the analysts' role in the capitalist system. He used a classic "4 why's" method (i.e., keep asking "why?" until you can't go any deeper).

1. Why does Sanford Bernstein exist? *To provide superior global research*
2. Why? *To know more and make better decisions*
3. Why? *To create better long-term performance*
4. Why? *To provide peace of mind for our clients*

The roomful of 300 analysts was provided with a deeply satisfying reason for the importance of their work.

Another source of powerful purpose thinking is the 300 Club,[10] a global alliance of CIOs interested in defining a noble future for the industry. On their website and in their white papers, they assert that the investment industry must go beyond the simple goal of making money for their clients—which is, of course, important—to the broader goal of investing in such a way that the cumulative effect of investing doesn't create a net loss for the planet.[11] For example, if certain companies are earning a good return but damaging the environment in the process, then society may incur a net loss as it later cleans up the mess. The movement toward socially responsible investing, such as ESG, is a sign that the consciousness of the industry is embracing this notion.

Motivation Beyond Purpose

Purpose is important to investment firms because it motivates employees and contributes to a strong culture. Purpose is considered an "intrinsic" motivator. It provides motivation within an individual, as opposed to, say, money, which is an external motivator. Both can be used to motivate, but the intrinsic motivators tend to be more powerful and more sustainable. In fact, in FCG's research, we find that purpose, while important, is by no means the most powerful intrinsic motivator. The chart in Table 1.3 indicates that autonomy and passion are even more important.

Table 1.3 Intrinsic Motivators

Motivate me by giving me more...	
Autonomy	17.6%
Passion for the Work	16.0%
Purpose/Meaning	15.6%
Bonuses	14.8%
Continuous Improvement	13.5%
Winning/Competition	13.1%
Status	5.7%
Emotional Pressures	3.7%

Leadership clearly involves motivating staff members, so let's expand on this notion of intrinsic versus extrinsic. Four big factors for both types of motivation are shown in Table 1.4.

Table 1.4 Motivation Factors

Extrinsic	Intrinsic
• Emotional pressures • Bonuses • Status • Winning and competition	• Doing something important • Believing in what you do • Doing it because it's right • Doing it because you love it

Extrinsic motivators are carrots and sticks. They represent external influences that attract or repel. Bonuses attract. Threatening bosses repel. Conversely, intrinsic motivators—aptly named—are independent of influences outside of us. When we do meaningful work, we are naturally self-motivated. When we do the right thing, virtue is its own reward. When we love our work, we thrive. Ideally, doing purposeful work that we love is as good as it gets.

So, which is more effective in obtaining investment success: extrinsic or intrinsic? The *Phi* study,[12] mentioned earlier, revealed that a 1% increase in phi—based on a diagnostic the study authors created—is associated with:

- 28% greater odds of excellent organizational performance
- 55% greater odds of excellent client satisfaction
- 57% greater odds of excellent employee engagement

There you have it: more success and more engagement when intrinsic motivators are at work. What actions can investment leaders take to build intrinsic motivation in their firm? The actions listed in Table 1.5 are good examples.

Table 1.5 Motivating Actions

Action	Industry Data
Articulate a compelling vision.	Only 44% of investment professionals believe that their leaders do this.
Remind staff of their fiduciary duty.	Only 46% of retail investors believe that financial institutions operate in the client's best interest.
Create an inspirational statement of purpose (a mission statement that explains the "why" for the firm).	Only 5% of managers believe their mission statement has a significant positive influence on the day-to-day lives of their employees.
Teach and coach employees.	Only 33% of investment professionals believe this is occurring at their firm.

Others include:

- Aligning staff with work they love to do
- Developing a set of core values that is meaningful to the staff
- Connecting the goals of the firm to purpose
- Providing staff members with autonomy: how, when, and where they do their work
- Encouraging and supporting continuous learning

Future leaders of investment firms would be wise to shift their mindsets from extrinsic to intrinsic motivators. Otherwise, they risk losing valuable talent. So, step away from the carrots and sticks … and bring on the purpose, autonomy, and mastery.

---

2   FCG's research on "meaningful aspects of work" reveals that the top five reasons (in order) are: 1) the work itself, 2) clients, 3) colleagues, 4) financial gain, 5) larger purpose.

3   See the Edelman Trust Barometer at http://www.edelman.com/insights/intellectual-property/2016-edelman-trust-barometer/

4   Millennials were born from 1981 1996; baby baby boomers from 1946 to 1964.

5   Michael Falk, *Let's All Learn How to Fish…To Sustain Long-Term Economic Growth* (2016). Available online at https://www.cfapubs.org/doi/abs/10.2470/rf.v2017.n1.5 and at Michael's home page: www.letsalllearnhowtofish.com (free). Also available as a webinar offered by FCG: www.focuscgroup.com

6   https://en.wikipedia.org/wiki/Hippocratic_Oath

7   FCG's work in compensation, led by Keith Robinson, has given us ample opportunity to see the "money issues" up close and personal. Many focus on "only" getting a $1 million bonus, rather than the joy of doing work they love at huge income levels, i.e. higher than 99% of the world's workforce! We often let money become a big dissatisfier.

8   Daniel Pink, *Drive* (Riverhead Books, 2011), p. 54.

9   Duncan, *Discovering Phi*.

10   www.the300club.org

11   Such a paper can be found at their website: Saker Nusseibeh, "The Why Question" (March 2017), https://www.the300club.org/wp-content/uploads/2017/03/300-Club-COMMENTARY-0217-The-why-question-Saker-Nusseibeh-FINAL-060317.pdf

12   Duncan, *Discovering Phi*.

CHAPTER 2

Leadership: A Necessary Nuisance

T his chapter is by no means a comprehensive education on executive leadership (nor is this book, for that matter). Rather, it provides insights and tips for investment people who are in a leadership role … often under protest.

If for some unfathomable reason, you do want to dive more deeply into leadership, then a good place to start is Dave Ulrich's book, *The Leadership Capital Index*.[13] Investors will relate to it because the book aims to develop metrics for evaluating leaders, so that management teams can be assessed by (you guessed it) investors. I like Ulrich because he researches the topic and provides summaries of common ground shared by experts like Bennis, Blanchard, Drucker, Charan, Goldsmith, and the like. I find autobiographical accounts of leadership rather useless because one size does *not* fit all. Further, any single expert such as the ones just named is biased by her or his experience and personality type, so that person will have a distorted view. Ulrich synthesizes the literature well. (Lord knows how he wades through countless books on leadership. I have a whole shelf full of un-read leadership books. Twain: "Classics are the books that everyone owns but no one has read.")

Ulrich summarizes the key elements as shown in Figure 2.1.

Figure 2.1 Elements of Leadership

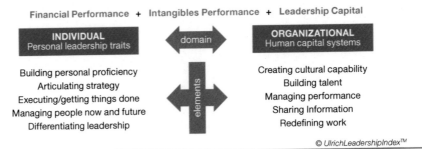

© UlrichLeadershipIndex™

A firm should be valued based on financial performance, intangibles, and the quality of leadership. We'll look at the latter.

Assessing Investment Leaders

Shifting from general industry to the investment world, here is a peek at FCG's experience assessing investment leaders.

Any self-respecting leader should want to know: How am I doing? So, do you know your strengths? Weaknesses? Do you know your blindspots? (Okay, that last one's a trick question.) Mayor Koch of New York City made this line famous: "How'm I doin'?" Koch's instincts were spot-on: get real-time feedback.

FCG advocates for feedback-rich environments, especially for leaders. FCG's process is a bit more formal than Mayor Koch's. We use a 360-feedback assessment.[14] This process allows leaders to get a "report card" on their leadership. It's remarkable how many investment leaders have *never* been formally assessed. The same leaders who advocate careful, thoughtful, logical analysis of investment strategies show none of that same concern in relation to their own leadership abilities. Apparently, the fact that they've become leaders is evidence enough that they are fully qualified and not in need of any further development.

Ri-i-ight.

This lack of curiosity is astounding. The ego of some investment leaders is world class—it would be amusing if it weren't so harmful. We worked with one senior PM who was viewed by all as a poor leader.[15] (Although, in fairness, he had an excellent performance record.) Analysts feared him and dreaded his meetings. They routinely left the firm, even without job prospects. So, when the CEO of the firm insisted that this PM undergo an assessment of his leadership abilities, he let forth a great outcry of whining and complaining, worthy of a mighty high-chair tyrant. The PM made sounds like a pig stuck in a fence. In fact, he resisted so violently that FCG finally relented and allowed him to pick his own raters—not a normal practice for 360 reviews (no stacking the deck …).

Eventually, FCG administered the 360 process with his "chosen friends-and-family raters" and then compiled the results. Despite coming from these hand-picked raters, the results were still embarrassingly low. (Think about this for a second: He got to "stack the deck" in his favor, and the results were *still* horrible. In a way that's impressively bad.) Admittedly, he earned high scores in "technical skills" (i.e., picking stocks), but the remaining scores for skills such as listening, encouraging teamwork, self-awareness, delegation, and so on would make Kim Jong Un or Robert Mugabe look good. However, this PM spared himself the pain of actually seeing the poor results by ignoring them entirely. True story. I pushed the report across the table to him, and he looked at it like it was a fresh turd. I began to debrief it with him, and he never touched the report. Instead, he delivered a tirade about FCG's stupid process, his lame team, and the ungrateful clients. It's safe to say that this PM is not our poster child for curiosity.

(All that said, I make it a practice to appreciate all the people we work with. In this case, the PM genuinely cared about creating value for the clients, and did so. That was praiseworthy.)

Interesting that these same "macho" PMs who strut about the firm with their BSDs[16] actually are quite cowardly.[17] They rationalize ignoring the assessment exercise because it is:

1. Stupid
2. Ill-conceived
3. Inaccurate
4. Useless
5. All of the above

But we all know the real reason: they're afraid. Their arrogance is just a big façade to protect their fragile egos. (Cue Jack Nicholson: "You can't handle the truth!")

So, let's flip this scenario. Consider a firm with excellent leadership. FCG has found some. The two leaders at this firm stepped directly into the challenge of being assessed with no hesitation. Their thinking was, "If I'm asking my senior team to be evaluated—and they were—then I'm going to lead the way. I won't ask them to do something that I won't do." Now *that* is leadership. Lead by example. No surprise, the results for the two senior leaders at this firm were off-the-charts good. We usually list the top five skillsets and the bottom five for each leader in the executive summary of the report (a standard strengths and weaknesses analysis). For these two leaders, we had to list more than 20 skills as "strong suits" because on a 5-point scale, their high scores were all tied at 4.9! Small wonder that this firm is so successful, even in these difficult markets. It is led brilliantly by these two senior people. The scores for the remaining 11 senior leaders were also good. Is this team perfect? Heavens no. Leadership teams, like families, are never perfect. They all have issues. But this team addresses them.

What distinguishes good leaders is their willingness to take the first step: *diagnose*. They are willing to take a good look in the mirror and see their reflection: the good, the bad, and the ugly.[18]

This look in the mirror then allows them to take the second step: *discovery*. Once you have collected the data, then you can intelligently analyze them and discover: Where am I strong? Where am I weak? And, importantly, where are my blindspots? Each of the participants in the leadership assessment had "ah-ha" moments regarding these insights. Some had hidden strengths, like "strategic thinking," that they were unaware of. We call these positive blindspots. Others had weaknesses, such as "delegates well," which surprised them. Negative blindspots. The goal of the 360 exercise is to arrive at a much clearer view of oneself as a leader. *How am I perceived?* Of course, we all wake up in the morning with good intentions about our professional duties. The problem is that intentions do not always equal impact. The only way to gauge the slippage or discrepancy is an assessment process.

The final step is *development*. Discovery leads to some good candidates for development. In this regard, the person doing the debriefing must be skillful. Too often, the participants look for the weakest scores and decide, "Gee, I should get busy improving my attention to detail. I'm really weak at that." Well, maybe. But FCG has had the most success with the following approach. Divide a person's skillsets into three broad buckets (Table 2.1).

Table 2.1 Skill Level Descriptions

Level of Skill	Description	Energy Factor
A skills ("genius")	The person has towering strengths in these areas and should use them a lot and continually look to improve upon them even more.	Very high. When doing these activities the individual is energized.
B skills ("excellent")	The person is excellent or very good at these skills. Better than most and recognized for them.	Neutral. When doing these activities the individual is neither energized or drained.
C skills ("weak")	The person is weak or at best competent in the skills. Typically does not like doing these activities.	Draining. These activities are not enjoyable an tend to drain energy.

These lower "C" skills are candidates for delegation; rarely does the strategy of working to improve them really pay off. In the preceding example about detail work, the leader should develop a strategy in which someone who *is* skilled at dealing with details can double-check the leader's work and supply that skill for him.

If leaders are clever about how they organize the tasks on their teams, they will familiarize themselves with this approach and then assign tasks accordingly. After a round of leadership assessments, FCG has facilitated the following exercise. All the team's tasks are written on sticky notes and placed on a wall. Then the leader asks team members to grab tasks that are high energy and high competence for them. In other words, "I like this task and I'm really good at it." In many trials, we've never seen a bunch of unclaimed stickies. Occasionally, there will be one or two odious tasks that no one wants, but that's rare. One person's poison is another's pleasure. Typically, all the tasks get chosen. Clearly, this is the most efficient way to allocate work. Each task gets allocated to the people who (1) like it and (2) excel at it.

So, as part of the development phase of assessments, we ask leaders to design a work schedule that allows them to spend 80% of their time in their areas of "genius" (i.e., high energy/high skill areas). Proper allocation of time is critical to high performance. Assessments can be hugely valuable in confirming areas of genius or uncovering hidden ones.

Strengths and weaknesses across all investment leaders are shown in Table 2.2.

Table 2.2 Investment Leaders Strengths and Weaknesses

Firm Competencies	Team Competencies	Self Competencies
Drive to win	Business processes	Perseverance
Critical thinking	Problem solving	Integrity and trust
Client focus	Continuous improvement	Functional/technical skills
Ethical/values centered	Planning effectively	Action-oriented
Drives firm vision	Conflict resolution	Comfort with higher managers
Asset management expertise	Work/life balance	Time management
Effective decision making	Delegates work to others	Self-motivated
Builds firm talent	Reading people	Candor
Strategic thinking	Builds effective collaboration	Listens actively
Servant leadership	Developing others	Self-awareness

Clearly, investment leaders do some things well, as highlighted in the green area. The weaknesses are shown in red. For each of these weaknesses, a relevant question is: *Does it matter?* As stated earlier, the development strategy used by FCG advocates leveraging strengths. Think carefully about what is important to your role—and what is realistic. As a team leader I may be weak in "developing others." Well, can someone else play that role? If I am the CIO, can my Director of Research cover that responsibility? Or take another competency: strategic thinking. Some people are natural strategists. They like it, and they are good at it. Others, not so much. It may be a huge waste of time to invest in raising someone's strategic skills when the firm doesn't need that person to do that. There are plenty of others who can fill that role around the leadership table.

So, do the leaders in your firm have the courage and curiosity to take an honest look at themselves? Do you? FCG's experience in this regard has been universally positive, if the leaders are genuinely committed to learning and developing. Again, the adversary in this situation is our old friend: Ego. Fearful and suspicious by nature, the Ego does *not* want to be placed under the bright lights. That would be terrible. The Ego thinks: "I could be exposed as a fraud! I could be far less wonderful than I think I am! I could be forced to admit my shortcomings! I could be vulnerable!" And because the Ego doesn't trust anyone, the thought of being exposed or becoming vulnerable is untenable: It must be avoided at all costs. "Hunker down, stay under your rock, be safe" is the advice of the Ego to all leaders.

So, who are you listening to? Your Ego, or your Better Self. If you haven't been formally assessed in many years, then it is the Ego. And the Ego loves your willful blindness! Keep pretending that it's okay to do nothing. Just as you:

A. Don't maintain your car
B. Don't brush your teeth
C. Don't get medical checkups

Oh, wait. You DO do those things, right? Well then, why wouldn't you get your leadership checked out? You get the idea.

Hence, a logical and important question for leaders is: who keeps you honest?

Who Keeps You Honest?

We all have an Ego, and that means we all avoid tough feedback. I offer this antidote to willful blindness[19]: **Someone who keeps you honest**. In many client engagements, FCG will ask the CEO this question, "Who keeps you honest?" Sometimes the question is met with a quizzical stare, and the response, "What do you mean?" So, we explain that everyone needs a person who will call us on our BS. Given the nature of willful blindness, we need someone who is not afraid of us and who is quite willing to challenge our thinking (or lack thereof).

FCG's experience shows that many CEOs do *not* have someone who keeps them honest. Like Warren Buffett, we all need a Charlie Munger to call foul. If I go through my mental Rolodex and picture CEOs who don't have a "BS whistleblower," there is a common denominator: Ego. Insecurity and Ego are opposite sides of the same coin. The biggest Egos that we've experienced at FCG are masking the greatest insecurities.

Andrew Lo (of MIT) wrote a piece in which he commented on willful blindness and how it leads to disastrous consequences.[20] Lo uses the fictional character Gordon Gekko to illustrate how Ego-driven, greedy leaders can create toxic cultures. Lo then asks, what is the best way to immunize against the Gekko effect? Lo's answer is:

> The psychologist Philip Zimbardo [who did the prison-guard experiment at Stanford[21]] put the answer succinctly: resist situational influences. Zimbardo was lucky enough to have a dissenting opinion [his wife!] that he implicitly trusted before his prison experiment spiraled out of control. Since that time, Zimbardo has investigated how good people can be influenced into doing evil things by their surrounding culture, much as the character Bud Fox was seduced by Gordon Gekko's culture in "Wall Street."[22]

What Lo—and Zimbardo—are saying is that situations can influence us to behave poorly, so we all need a reality check. We need someone we trust—possibly outside the environment—who can give us candid feedback about our decisions and behavior. Zimbardo's list of antidotes to willful blindness includes:

1. Someone who will keep us honest
2. Willingness to admit our mistakes
3. Willingness to challenge authority
4. Ability to prioritize the future over the immediate present (e.g., instant gratification)
5. Adherence to the values of honesty, responsibility, and independence of thought

Returning to the first antidote, ask yourself: "When was the last time someone blew the BS whistle on me?" For many of us, the answer is a long, long time! Maybe when we were in grade school and told the teacher, "My dog ate my homework"—and we got busted for telling a lame whopper. Some CEOs are still telling whoppers and going bust-free.

Zimbardo rightly identifies "situational influences" as the real culprit in willful blindness. I confess to sitting in more than one strategy session in which I said nothing while the leadership team discussed ways to push questionable products on unsuspecting clients. Why was I silent? Situational influence. It seemed so uncomfortable to speak my conscience when the whole room was aligned around the "vibe" of sell, sell, sell. As if I would be the world's biggest spoilsport to ruin everyone's fun. (Frank Burns in *MASH*, the classic wet blanket. [Millennials: ask your boomer co-worker.]) And, of course, remember Sinclair Lewis's wonderful advice: "It is difficult to get a man to understand something when his salary depends upon him not understanding it."[23]

Obviously, interfering with someone's income is never a popular choice.[24]

Assuming you have the wisdom and courage to welcome a bona-fide BS whistleblower into your life, how do you avoid situational influences? Very simply, work around them. In other words, don't expect your "keep-you-honest" partner to operate in public settings, like staff meetings. Instead, meet with him or her privately and solicit feedback.[25] Ask specifically, "What possible blindspots did I have in that meeting?" Note, the question is not "Did I have any blindspots?" because that makes it too easy to receive a one-word answer: no. Rather, assume that you have a blindspot—we all do—and ask for feedback on what it looks like.

A common blindspot that FCG observes is *blaming*. Most investment leaders recognize that blame is toxic in organizations.[26] But then they subtly—or not so subtly—turn around and blame someone in a staff meeting. If you have an honesty partner, she or he can provide feedback after the meeting. This awareness would then allow you to use Zimbardo's #2 antidote: admit your mistake. Far too many leaders allow their egos to tell them not to admit mistakes. Why? It makes you look weak. One of my favorite TV heroes, Jethro Gibbs on NCIS, is guilty of this same stupid advice to his team: *Rule 6: "Never say you're sorry. It's a sign of weakness."*[27]

This may be one of the dumbest "rules" operative in the corporate world. We are all human and we all make mistakes, so why pretend that we don't? Let's all get this one straight: appropriate apologies are a sign of maturity, humility, and respect. Not weakness.

Of course, if your career is an unending series of apologies, then something else is wrong. That's different. We are talking about the occasional, sincere apology when you screwed up. In FCG's experience, the willingness to take responsibility for a mistake—and apologize—is nearly always met with appreciation. People realize it takes courage to apologize.

So, what are we suggesting here? A simple checklist:

1. Establish someone in your professional life who keeps you honest (your own personal BS whistleblower).
2. Acknowledge that you have blindspots and ask your BS whistleblower to point them out.
3. Do this in private, so that situational influences don't overpower the whistleblower.
4. When you get feedback that you have screwed up, admit your mistake; when appropriate, apologize.

This seems simple enough. So, why don't we do it? *Ego.* (Are you picking up on a theme here?) The simple prescription discussed here is the *last* thing that Ego wants. Ego loves to be in control, to look good, and to be right. Ego hates humility. Ego is constantly on the lookout for whistleblowers, so that it can root them out and crush them. If Ego reads this chapter it will tell you, "This is the dumbest thing you've read all week. Ignore it!"

Of course, many readers will react to this advice by thinking, "I don't need this coaching, but so-and-so definitely does!" Okay, first off, ask your BS whistleblower if that is really true: i.e., that you don't need this coaching! Then, if you must, photocopy this piece (you have my permission) and leave it on so-and-so's desk, with the appropriate parts underlined!

Meantime, I want to thank my whistleblowers:[28] my business partners, who don't seem at all afraid to call me on my BS. (Clearly, I have been way too lenient in my leadership …) And my ultimate whistleblower, my wife. She is not the least bit intimidated by me. I can't get away with anything.

Character of a Leader

The old line that "leaders should *have* character, not *be* characters" is especially true in the investment world. Given how many leaders FCG has worked with, we know that many of them are both. In a way, that's good news because it means they do have character, in the positive sense. Unfortunately, too many leaders in our industry do *not* care about leadership character. As noted, they often don't care much about leadership, period! For many, if a person gets results, that's what counts.

Fred Kiel's book, *Return on Character*[29] is excellent in this regard. It's a sequel to his first book, called *Moral Intelligence*,[30] in which he discussed what he believes are the four core values of a person who has character:

1. **Integrity:** words and actions align. A person of integrity makes and keeps clear agreements. They are persons of their word. (For more on integrity, see the essay in Appendix A of this book.)
2. **Responsibility:** conscientious behavior. They take responsibility for their lives, their actions, and the consequences. They don't blame others. They are concerned for the common good.
3. **Compassion:** living with empathy. They can put themselves in another's place. They genuinely care about people. They look for win/win outcomes.
4. **Forgiveness:** understanding that we are human, we all make mistakes. They ease up on perfectionism. They cultivate the skill of "letting go." They give themselves and others a second chance, a fresh start.

Kiel is 75 years old and has been studying and thinking about the character of leaders for three decades. He's getting the hang of this subject. In his book, he has carefully researched "the inextricable link between CEO character and value creation." He calls the leaders of high character "Virtuoso CEOs" and the leaders who scored lower in the surveys (taken by employees) "Self-Focused CEOs." As Kiel's study shows:

> There is an observable and consistent relationship between character-driven leaders and better business results. Leaders with stronger morals and principles do, in fact, deliver a Return on Character (ROC). Leaders that rank high on the ROC character-assessment scale achieve nearly **five times** the return on assets that leaders who fall at the bottom of the curve achieve.[31]

So, how is *character* defined? Here is Kiel's working definition: "an individual's unique combination of internalized beliefs and moral habits that motivate and shape how that individual relates to others."

Interestingly, the study reveals a huge blindspot for the Self-Focused CEOs: they rate themselves just as highly on the character-assessment scale as the Virtuoso CEOs. Think about that for a moment. The bad leaders delude themselves into thinking they are every bit as virtuous as the good ones!

The scores are shown in Table 2.3.

Table 2.3 Comparison of CEOs Self-Ratings vs. Employee Ratings of the CEOs

Character scores for:	Self-rating	Employee rating of CEO
Self-Focused CEOs	83	68
Virtuoso CEOs	84	87

Note that the employee ratings of Virtuoso CEOs is even higher than those CEOs' self-ratings. Modesty seems to be another trait of character-driven leaders! Obviously, these results speak to the importance of objective feedback for all of us. As described earlier, FCG runs 360-feedback surveys on many investment leaders to help them get beyond their biases and see a more objective picture of themselves.

For Kiel, character is both nature and nurture. The combination of life experiences and the person's DNA determine character principles and habits. Fortunately, the plasticity of the brain allows us to improve our character at any stage in life. Through accurate feedback from colleagues and friends, we can assess how we are doing on the core four character traits: integrity, responsibility, compassion, and forgiveness. To the extent we are weak in one area, we can address it and improve it. The research from Kiel shows that this effort is well worth it. Because *who we are* as leaders matters greatly. Character counts.

The second aspect of leadership involves what leaders do. A key aspect of FCG's consulting approach is to make things "crayon simple." In the case of leadership, the crayon-simple statement is: *Good leadership consists of WHO you are, and WHAT you do.* Kiel's work on the "WHO" piece is very useful in this regard, but he also describes what leaders do.

Specifically, good leaders do the following:

- They create and communicate compelling **visions of success** (what does the future look like?)
- They create clear **strategies** for realizing the vision of success (How will we get there?)
- They **execute** on their plans (How will we make things happen?)

In this way, Kiel's book dovetails nicely with the work of Ulrich. Ulrich writes, "All leaders must excel at personal proficiency. Without the foundation of trust and credibility, you cannot ask others to follow you."[32] In Ulrich's leadership self-assessment, one of the items is "I model character and integrity." In contrast to Kiel, though, Ulrich is much more interested in defining and describing the "what" rather than the "who" of leadership.

The reassuring overlap between these two authors is twofold:

1) Kiel and Ulrich agree that good leaders must have character, with integrity and trust as core components of "character."
2) They also overlap nicely on what leaders must do. Kiel and Ulrich both emphasize vision, strategy, and execution.

In addition to these key overlaps, Ulrich emphasizes:

- **Talent management.** Leaders identify, build, and engage talent to get results now
- **Building the next generation.** Leaders create succession plans to ensure future success

Kiel adds three additional capabilities that leaders must excel at:

- **Decision making.** Good leaders must make good decisions. (This one seems so obvious, and yet many leadership experts don't spend much time discussing it.)
- **Creating a culture of accountability.** This draws on the character traits of integrity and responsibility. Good leaders spell out expectations and boundaries so that employees have clear guidelines, including an awareness of consequences for violating those boundaries. (See Chapter 7 on accountability for more on this important topic.)
- **Building a strong executive team.** The CEO must select qualified individuals who share the core character values (integrity, responsibility, compassion, forgiveness) and build them into a high-performing team.

The Focus Elite firms[33] that FCG selects and studies all have highly functioning executive committees ("ExCos"). The chart in Table 2.4 compares the Focus Elite ExCos with the industry average. All the differences are significant at the 99% confidence level.

Table 2.4 Success Factors for Top ExCos

Team Factors	Focus Elite	Industry	Difference
I feel fairly **compensated** for my contributions	5.99	5.18	0.81
We have the right **team members** to accomplish our goals	6.15	5.41	0.75
There is a high level of **trust** among team members	5.98	5.30	0.68
Our team openly **debates** issues	5.79	5.21	0.58
As a team we value and **appreciate** one another	6.08	5.55	0.53

7 point scale: 7 = strongly agree, 1 = strongly disagree

Note that selecting the right team members and building high trust levels are critically important to a high-functioning ExCo. Kiel writes, "To achieve Virtuoso-level results, leaders need A-level executives on their team from the start. It's better to have a temporary vacancy on the team than to tolerate a player with mediocre skills or weak character habits. [FCG calls these people Red Xs (see Chapter 6.] A lackluster senior executive team will eventually fail or, at best, achieve only modest results."[34] FCG agrees. In fact, the quickest way to build a strong culture is to build a strong Executive Committee. CEOs often ask us about building culture and our crayon-simple answer is: build a great ExCo. The positive effects will cascade throughout the organization.

So, how are investment firms doing at building great ExCos? Not so well. Table 2.5 shows a voting slide from a group of CFAs who attended an FCG presentation. Note that the results for this audience mirror the global results (11 CFA societies) of 43%.

Table 2.5 Executive Committee Building

We have anExCo of six or less qualified members that leads our firm well	
Agree	43%
Neutral	18%
Disagree	39%

Again, asset management firms still don't take leadership very seriously. Results like the one in Table 2.5 provide ample evidence that investment technicians still believe they can lead the business, without the desire or training necessary to do so. Interestingly, the younger generations—Xers and Yers—are voicing the message, with increasing volume, that they want to be trained and developed as leaders. Also, FCG is getting more requests to help firms meet these mentoring demands. In response, we have created a curriculum to develop "good enough" leaders. This term is borrowed from the parenting expression: "good enough" parenting. Because parenting—and leadership—are not exact sciences, the idea is to do the job well enough so that your kids—or employees—can succeed. Put differently, if you are "good enough," your influence is at worst neutral!

So, if you are interested in becoming a good-enough leader, consider the advice from Kiel: concentrate on the four core values that define character. Then ask yourself, Have I built a good senior team? And have we clearly defined our vision and strategy? Remember, it's okay to *be* a character if you *have* character. And now you know what character is: integrity, responsibility, compassion, and forgiveness. It's so simple ... and it only took me five decades to figure it out.

Clear Leadership

Clarity is a passion of mine, and should be for leaders as well. My colleagues at FCG will tell you that I go into spasms when a client responds to something we said with, "Huh? I don't understand what you mean." Argh! I tell my colleagues repeatedly, "That's the worst thing we can hear!" Our job at FCG is to bring clarity to a client's confusion. We help them sort out the issues and make good decisions. Bringing more confusion to a client is like a doctor bringing more sickness to a patient. First, do no harm! Or, in our case: Don't add to the confusion! Leaders should have the same concern: provide order and clarity, not more confusion.

So, I was delighted when a client recommended a book called *Clear Leadership*.[35] The tie-in with our work was the chapter in the book about appreciation. The author, Gervase Bushe, promotes appreciation as a powerful way to unleash the potential of an organization, as does FCG. Beyond advocating for appreciation, Bushe is excellent on the topic of clarity. He argues that much of the communication in firms is "mush." That's our experience at FCG as well. In Bushe's words:

> *Interactions between people are based on stories they've made up about each other that they haven't checked out directly with the other person. I call this condition "interpersonal mush," and I am convinced that collaboration is not sustainable in interpersonal mush.*[36]

To form a successful partnership with colleagues, one must eliminate mush. Bushe defines *partnership* as "a relationship between two or more people who are jointly committed to the success of whatever process or project they are engaged in."[37] For senior teams (e.g., ExCos), FCG would simplify it to "a relationship between two or more people who are jointly committed to the success of their shared mission."

To be successful in partnership, Bushe says that four skillsets are necessary:

1. Self-awareness (Emotional Intelligence)
2. Descriptiveness (candor and transparency)
3. Curiosity (mutual understanding)
4. Appreciation (identifying and amplifying the strengths)

For those of you who have followed FCG's work closely, you realize that this is exactly what we've been preaching for more than 15 years. When I first described *Clear Leadership* to Keith Robinson, FCG's managing partner, with perky and animated excitement, he looked puzzled and asked, "Did you learn anything new?" His question gave me pause. Hmmm. Was I just excited because Bushe was affirming all our belief systems? Partly, yes. But Bushe has also added some good concepts and techniques to the toolkit. For example, Bushe introduces what he calls the "cube," which captures the four important elements of one's experience in a conversation:

Table 2.6 Conversation Cube

Observing: What are the facts? What can we all agree on or agree to?	**Thinking:** What story did you make up about the facts? What is your opinion, evaluation, judgment?
Wanting: What is it that you want? What does a successful outcome look like?	**Feeling:** What is your reaction to the story? Does it evoke anger, sadness, joy, fear …?

For clear communication to occur, it is very helpful to master the cube. Much of the "mush" in communication occurs because people don't understand the distinctions. For example, people confuse observations (facts) with thinking (stories). Consider each of the following statements and pick out the observations:

- I observe that you are upset.
- I observe that he is hungry.
- I observe her working hard.

None of these statements is an observation! They are all thoughts (stories) about someone's behavior. As Bushe writes, "to get clear, you need to be able to tell the difference between what you think, feel, want and observe."[38] FCG's advice in this regard is to know the difference between fact and story, and then to hold your story lightly (because it is only your opinion, not the final Truth). Further, both FCG and Bushe argue for the importance of checking out your story. For example, FCG was with a CEO who said, "I'm irritated that David was in Boston and was too lazy to go visit our big client." Keith and I both jumped on that one: "Have you checked out your story with David?" The CEO's response: "No." Untold damage occurs on teams (and in marriages) when we run with our stories instead of checking them out. Bushe and FCG both argue that this is where curiosity plays a big role. Instead of getting judgmental ("David is lazy"), get curious: why did David not visit our client? (In this case, the CEO did check out his story later and found that David had indeed called the client to schedule a meeting, but the client was unavailable!)

Bushe suggests that good transparency on a team would mean that each team member could skillfully provide a description (i.e., the descriptive skills) of an event from all four quadrants of the cube. In the preceding case, the CEO might say, "I observe that David did not visit our client in Boston. My story is that he's lazy. I'm irritated by that. Because I want our clients to receive world-class treatment from our firm." This would be an accurate description of what the CEO was experiencing in the here-and-now. Anyone listening would know where the CEO was coming from. In this case, a good suggestion from a colleague would be, "Check out your story." Teams that learn and practice this behavior eliminate much of the mush in their conversations, and reduce a great deal of drama.

The final quadrant of the cube, the "Wants" piece, is also useful in cutting through mush. Instead of guessing what people want, teach the team to state it explicitly. Bushe writes, "One rule of partnership is that people have to say what they want. The second rule is that they shouldn't expect to get it."[39]

We practice this rule often at FCG. We state what we want—"I request such-and-such"— and then allow team members to comply or not. For example, my request of team members is that they turn off their smartphones when we meet. If they do so, great. If not, well, that's their business. At least I've made my request clearly. (Note: When we talk about requests, we are not talking about things like embezzling from the firm: "Please don't steal our money." That's not a request, that should be an agreement with your partners!)

Another way to cut through mush is to use clear language. Be precise. Bushe writes, "If someone enters the room and feels cold, he is most likely to say, 'it's cold in here.' Coldness is a sensation, an inner experience. I have canvassed rooms of people and found that some are cold, some are hot, and some are neither."[40] When we get the hang of this precision in language, we stop making statements like "this is a fun company to work for." Instead, we make an accurate statement such as "I have fun working here."

(Whether other people do or do not have fun is uncertain.) Owning one's experience and making "I" statements can really help with clarity. I was with a CIO who said, "When you go and look at the stocks they've put in my portfolio, you just want to scream about the mess they've made. We've worked really hard to improve the process, but you look at their attitude and just have to shake your head."

Obviously, the CIO is the one who just wants to scream and shake his head. The "you" language is so prevalent that most of us have learned to translate it when we hear it. But who is the "we" that has worked so hard to improve the process? It turns out it was the CIO, but that wasn't obvious until I asked. Bushe writes, "The rule of clear language is very simple—say 'I' when you are talking about your own experience."[41]

FCG would add that pronouns can get very complicated as well. Instead of saying, "He was unwilling to share resources with her because he knew that she would get upset," say: "Paul was unwilling to share resources with Mary because Paul knew that Susan would get upset." This precision may seem a bit overdone, but it is well worth the effort because it eliminates confusion. Some common examples of the confusion:

- We need to take a break (when really, I need to take a break).
- We're glad you came (when really, I'm glad you came).
- It's scary to tell the boss the truth (when really, I'm scared to tell the boss the truth).

Bushe has some very useful and practical advice for leaders, such as "Make statements before asking questions." Hmmm, you might wonder. Why do that? Bushe gives this example:

> The boss says, "Do you support our plans or don't you?" This seems to be a straightforward question, but what kind of "story" will it generate in the listener? One might infer undertones of distrust. Another might begin trying to imagine why the question is being asked. A third might think that her reservations about the plans are clearly not welcome. Questions lead to more clarity all around only when they are preceded by descriptive statement. For example the boss could say, "Yesterday you seemed really committed to our plan when you were describing it to Sally, but today you keep hedging on your commitment. I'm feeling confused. Do you support our plans or don't you?" Make a statement before you ask the question.[42]

Bushe's book is full of these tips for clarity, which I love. Perhaps the most useful one is about candor. When FCG asks teams why they are less than fully candid, the most common response is: If I am fully candid, I might hurt someone's feelings. The underlying reality here is that most of us have been trained in one way or another to hold others responsible for our experience (i.e., you make me feel …). Bushe gives this example:

> Let's say you work for me, and you start to tell me that the plan we are executing is not going to work. I start to get anxious, and instead of listening to your concerns and delving more deeply into where they are coming from, I argue with you about why you are wrong and why the plan will work. Or maybe, instead of arguing, I give you a pep talk about how it will all work out if we stay the course, and ask you to get on board. In either case, I am trying to get you to have a different experience about the plan so I won't feel anxious. Rather than taking responsibility for creating my own experience (the anxiety), I'm implicitly making you responsible for my experience. You have to change so I won't feel anxious![43]

FCG witnesses this form of mush week after week. Team members are unwilling to be honest about their views because they might offend someone. The remedy is to discuss and agree as a team that each member is responsible for his or her own reactions—and that it is expected of team members to candidly state their views as objectively and respectfully as possible, regardless of how others react. This simple understanding and agreement could profoundly transform a team's conversations. I take responsibility for my reactions; you take responsibility for yours. Clear? Good. Now, can we talk … ?

Give the CEO a Break!

I've been slamming away at leaders throughout this chapter (and book), so I want to include a peace offering of support. It's hard to be a successful leader! No question. Even the best leaders we work with have a plateful of challenges to manage. Here, I describe the most frequent challenges and acknowledge the difficulty of the role. So, take heart, leaders: nobody gets it *all* right. Your mantra should be "progress over perfection."

Investment CEOs are easy choices for the Rodney Dangerfield "I-don't-get-no-respect" award. Despite long hours in a tough environment, they still get the lowest ratings from Edelman in the trust survey (Table 2.7).

Table 2.7 U.S. Informed Publics: Trust in Financial Sources

Broker/Advisor	68%
Friends or family	61%
Portfolio manager	55%
Corporate communications	44%
Host of a cable television show on investing	33%
CEO or other senior excecutives of a financial services company	32%

Source: Edelman trustbarometer

Ouch. CEOs rank even lower than "Hosts of a cable television show on investing" (read: Jim Cramer). I'm not here to defend all investment CEOs, because many of them do deserve bad ratings. But the CEOs with whom FCG deals are mainly good guys/gals with intact consciences, who are working hard to achieve the goals FCG described in a white paper called "The Investment Challenge."[44]

Keith and I met separately with two CEOs of larger organizations to review their firm's culture assessment. The purpose of these assessments is to help CEOs understand their current culture and then make decisions about follow-up steps. The data are collected via online survey (15 minutes) and face-to-face interviews with leaders (solo) and focus groups (5 to 8 people in the room). The report that we produce is massive—250 pages—and FCG's job is to highlight the key elements so that the information is both understandable and actionable. This is where this segment's title—give the CEO a break—comes into play. It's a big job with so many variables, and yet the staff comments (from the survey and the interviews) suggest that there is almost no appreciation on the part of staff for the magnitude of the challenge. My goal is to heighten appreciation of the fact that CEOs face a lot of really tough tradeoffs. If staff members understood this more fully, they might have a little compassion for the boss. It's the old: "if you think it's so easy, try it yourself!" Many of the complaining staff members would do a chest-grab pretty quickly if they assumed the role of CEO! (As one CIO said when he assumed the new role of CEO, "My confidence peaked the day of my promotion. After that it was all downhill!")

So, here are the seven toughest issues that came up in both debriefs:

1. Embracing and practicing "excellence/continuous improvement" as a value in the culture.
2. Understanding and responding to the demand for "leadership development/ mentoring" within each organization. What are new workers asking for?

3. Short-term versus long-term goals. No surprise here; all firms wrestle with this tradeoff.
4. Investment-centric versus sales-centric organization. Which leads and which follows?
5. Transparency. How much is enough? What does "open communication" mean?
6. Debate. Most firms wrestle with "polite/nice" winning out over "challenging/honest."
7. Flexibility. Work/life balance and flexible work arrangements are becoming ever more important.

Excellence/Continuous Improvement: The quest for finding an edge and staying ahead

Both firms in question identified this value—Excellence/Continuous Improvement—as a top aspirational value. In other words, the data suggest that we are not practicing it a lot now, but we should be! In some ways, CEOs should take comfort in the survey results because it is the *staff* telling them that we need to raise our game. The challenge for CEOs and the executive team is determining how to do it. Most firms are already putting in long hours, so that is not the answer (i.e., work harder). Rather, CEOs must become thoughtful and creative around specific techniques for improving productivity and results. One CEO in our debrief went immediately to meetings: "We spend a lot of time in meetings and it is not optimal." FCG promised to provide a "best practices" sheet for meetings. Basics include: Send an agenda in advance. Include the purpose and desired outcomes in the agenda. Describe pre-work that will allow attendees to be fully prepared.

Additionally, there is a growing body of research on continuous improvement with excellent books such as:[45]

- *The Talent Code* by Dan Coyle (Bantam, 2009)
- *Development of Professional Expertise* by K. Anders Ericsson (Cambridge University Press, 2009)
- *Mindset* by Carol Dweck (Ballantine Books, 2007)
- *Practice Perfect* by Doug Lemov (Jossey-Bass, 2012)
- *Outliers* by Malcolm Gladwell (Back Bay Books, 2011)
- *Getting Things Done* by David Allen (Penguin Books, 2015)

Each of these books offers great ideas about how to raise one's game. The subtitle of Lemov's book is "42 Rules for Getting Better at Getting Better." And the good news about getting better is that Dan Pink (in *Drive*[46]) reassures us that we want to get better naturally. He calls it the drive for mastery. As knowledge workers, we naturally want to perfect our craft. So, analysts don't need to be pushed and goaded into becoming better analysts. They just need guidance and mentoring as to *how*. Which brings us to the next thorny issue for CEOs: leadership development/mentoring.

Leadership Development/Mentoring: The quest for guidance and career planning

Look at the results from the two firms in our example, plus the Focus Elite (the nine firms that we track as excellent in culture) in Table 2.8.

Table 2.8 Culture Gap

Leadership Development/ Mentoring	% Responses for "aspirational culture"	% Responses for "existing culture"	Gap between Aspirational and Existing
Firm A	36%	9%	27%
Firm B	36%	2%	34%
Focus Elite firms (9)	28%	8%	20%

For the two firms (A and B) and for the Focus Elite, the gap between what they have and what they want is big—and these results are consistent with those from the industry at large. In fact, FCG has seen this gap so often that we've researched what staff members mean when they say, "we want more leadership development and mentoring." Table 2.9 shows a sample vote from a room of 30 staff members.

Table 2.9 Sample Leadership Development/Mentoring Vote

Which offerings would be attractive as "leadership development/mentoring/" (10 votes, spread over all options)	
Mentoring	77
Coaching	50
Career pathing	48
Equity Global Market Forums	33
Technical training	30
Leadership classes	28
Rotational assignments	28
Conferences	24
Internal workshops	18
Job challenges	2

Consistently, we see the three top vote-getters repeated in our data collection. Younger staff members want:

1. Clear career paths. What are the steps to the next level? How do I advance? What is the time frame? (FCG has borrowed from the martial arts and developed "belts" for various job categories such as analyst.)

2. Mentoring. How do I get assigned a mentor (who is not my boss) and who can help me learn and understand the ropes in this company?
3. Coaching. How do I get access to professional coaching (from an outside expert), who can help me learn and polish my leadership skills?

Smart CEOs—like the two we met with—are taking seriously this notion that younger workers want to be developed. In fact, one of the CEOs in question said, "This gap was the most surprising and important bit of information from the whole survey."

Short-Term vs. Long-Term: How does the firm balance these two time frames?
All businesses everywhere face this dilemma: balancing short- and long-term needs. In the investment industry it is particularly fierce because firms are under intense pressure to produce quarterly results. Both of our exemplar firms are public and therefore at the mercy of shareholders. Nevertheless, each CEO has done a good job of balancing short- and long-term concerns, as you can see in the survey results in Table 2.10.

Table 2.10 Short-Term vs. Long-Term Results

	Firm A	Firm B
Leaders seem focused on the short term results	35%	32%
Neutral	31%	13%
Leaders seem focused on the long term results	34%	55%

The blue and gold boxes show responses to the question concerning whether firm leaders are more focused on short- or long-term results. To their credit, these CEOs have avoided heavy "blue" voting. The staff is saying, "Our CEO has not caved in to the short-term pressures." They are balancing the demands of different masters.

Investment-Centric vs. Sales-Centric: Do leaders favor investment performance over asset gathering?
Here is another very tough balance that leaders must strike. The firms must grow their assets to keep shareholders happy and employees happy (with opportunities to advance in the firm), but they must also perform in order to keep clients happy. One story, related elsewhere in this book, sums up this friction. Over lunch I asked a CIO who had recently resigned if there was a critical moment in his decision. He said, "Yes. A client met with our CEO and offered to put $200 million to work in our flagship fund. I had told the CEO earlier that we could not accept any more funds into that portfolio without damaging

performance. Our CEO shook his head and told the client, "Sorry, that portfolio is capped.' Then the client said, 'How about $400 million?' And our CEO said, 'Done!' That was the last straw. He showed that he had no integrity around our investment process!" FCG acknowledges that both goals are legitimate: to perform well and to grow. We applaud the CEOs who have skewed the results toward performance over growth. In the case of the two firms we are highlighting, one met that standard, the other did not, as shown Table 2.11.

Table 2.11 Asset Gathering vs. Investment Performance

	Firm A	Firm B
Investment Team Leaders are mostly focused on asset gathering (sales-centric)	20%	38%
Neutral	12%	37%
Investment Team Leaders are mostly focused on fund performance (investment-centric)	68%	25%

Both are in an acceptable range, but the second one indicates a bias toward growing assets over providing performance. In fact, the CIO of that firm agrees that its flagship fund has gotten too big.

Transparency: Do we practice open communication with our staff?
In FCG's experience, we see repeatedly that open communication builds trust and performance over time. We are strong proponents of erring on the side of more transparency. Many investment cultures have remnants of the old "command-and-control" management style in their cultures. Wise CEOs develop a communication strategy that allows them to share all the important information with their staff, avoiding any sense that they are keeping secrets or operating on a need-to-know basis. Both firms in this review would benefit from more transparency, as shown in Table 2.12.

Table 2.12 Transparency

Transparency vs. Need to Know	Firm A	Firm B
Leaders seem to favor transparency and openness of information	49%	42%
Neutral	16%	15%
Leaders approach infomation on a "need to know" basis	35%	43%

Open and Productive Debate: Have leaders created a culture in which staff members are encouraged to challenge ideas, even of the leaders?

Great investment firms must be learning organizations. They must foster an environment where the Ego takes a back seat to learning and growing. Very few investment firms have achieved this higher standard. As you can see in the survey results in Tables 2.12 and 2.13, each of these firms can improve on this dimension.

Table 2.13 Challenging and Debate

Challenging vs. Polite	Firm A	Firm B
Team members frequently challenge each other, have open debates	53%	49%
Neutral	13%	22%
Team members are tactful and polite in their discussion, rarely debating	34%	29%

CEOs and their leadership teams must demonstrate candor among themselves and reward it in their staffs. It is human nature to play it safe, so staff members must see over and over that leaders reward taking a risk: namely, challenging the status quo. Mind you, language is very important. There is a huge difference between saying, "That's a dumb idea" and "I see it differently." The former is disrespectful, whereas the latter is not. Good leaders will frequently ask during a discussion, "Does anyone see it differently?" If no one speaks up, the leader could push it further by saying, "I'd like someone to play devil's advocate. Argue the other side of this view." If the group is still hesitant, then ask them to write down a different view. Once they've written it, ask: "Will someone share what they've written?" Too many leaders we know take the easy way out by blaming the staff members: "They don't have the courage to speak up!" Good CEOs accept the challenge of making it safe to have open debate. If your team is not having open debate, then get curious about why and how you can model, encourage, and foster open debate! Don't just blame the staff.

Flexible Work Environment: Are workers trusted to get results in whatever fashion they choose?

Increasingly, FCG sees that younger workers in firms want to be allowed the autonomy to work where they want, when they want, and how they want. As you can see in the survey results in Table 2.14, one of the firms we're highlighting has done a good job of giving staff members this autonomy, while the other has not.

Table 2.14 Autonomy in Work Environment

Face Time vs. Results Only	Firm A	Firm B
Leaders pay attention to facetime, i.e. number of hours in the office	46%	18%
Neutral	16%	14%
Leaders are focused on results only, i.e. employees have complete autonomy as to how they get their results	38%	68%

FCG recommends that firms move in the direction of this second firm: give employees clear instructions as to what is expected of them (i.e., goals), and then turn them loose to accomplish those goals. FCG further recommends weekly check-ins with each employee to monitor progress and make course corrections where needed. Dan Pink showed clearly[48] that knowledge workers (read: YOUR staff members) love autonomy. FCG has seen this repeatedly in high-performing firms. In fact, for many workers more autonomy has a cash value. Smart CEOs understand that staff members can be very happy at work if they are given lots of autonomy and appreciation combined with fair (not excessive) compensation packages. Many roles in the investment firm—analyst, PM, strategist, sales—lend themselves nicely to flexible arrangements. Aside from Pink's work, the authorities on this subject are Ressler and Thompson, who wrote *Why Work Sucks and How to Fix It*.[49]

So, consider giving your leaders a break. Could you handle these issues more skillfully? Do you appreciate the tough job they have?

Apparently not. In reading through the pages and pages of comments that accompany the survey results, we are struck by the lack of appreciation for leaders. We're not defending CEOs who flat-out stink. However, the two CEOs in this case are both smart, decent men who genuinely care about the future of their firms—and who have very tough decisions to make. Speaking just for myself, I know I would have a difficult time improving on the job that each of them is doing. Heck, I'd probably be hyperventilating by the end of the first day. So, give your leaders a break. You don't have to give them a big old bear hug, but don't bust their chops. And maybe—just maybe—give them a high five from time to time. I'm just sayin'...

From Good to Great

Let's push the preceding analysis a bit further with a case study. Here I describe an exemplary leader—Fred Martin at Disciplined Growth Investors (DGI), a Focus Elite firm—and his best-in-class culture with the two that I described earlier. My goal is not to embarrass the "lesser" firms (who are midway through the journey) but to encourage them that it is possible to reach the goal of "great." DGI has been working diligently over many years to strengthen and improve its culture. It didn't come easily. They've had their challenges. But Martin is committed to doing whatever it takes to achieve the dual success of: 1) excellent performance for the clients, and 2) excellent work environment (culture) for the employees. Fred believes that if you take good care of clients and employees, you will inevitably take good care of owners as well. (As Fred is the majority shareholder of DGI, he has a real interest in proving this theory true!) In this section, I describe DGI's culture results, compare them with those of the other two firms, and provide my explanation for why DGI has achieved success.

Let's start with some metrics. How have these three firms done based on the factors in Table 2.15?

Table 2.15 Success Factor Ratings

Factor	DGI	Firm A	Firm B	Industry Average (90 firms)
Coherence (How much do employees rally around same values? 100% is perfect.)	49%	35%	34%	40%
Sludge (How much bad behavior, such as gossip and blame, is in the culture? Lower is better.)	1%	15%	19%	10%
Effective Decision Making (Percent of staff that agrees the culture supports effecting decision making)	94%	64%	38%	69%
Loyalty/Engagement (3s and 4s on a 4 point scale)	100%	61%	74%	80%
Attract/Retain Top Talent (Percent of staff that agree the firm can attract and retain top talent)	94%	84%	90%	81%
Firm Success (Percent of staff rating firm in top quintile vs. competitors)	100%	66%	50%	60%

Coherence measures the strength of the culture. To what degree is the staff rallying around the same set of positive cultural values and behaviors? The highest possible score is 100%, meaning that the staff perfectly lines up around the same values/behaviors.

The highest score recorded by FCG is 63%. DGI scored significantly higher than the industry average, and higher than firms A and B.

Firms A and B are lower than the industry average because this was their first survey. The industry includes many firms that have been working on their culture and taken the culture survey several times. The average for first-timers such as A and B is 32%. What's needed to improve the score for A and B? Each CEO in concert with the executive committee must decide which values are core and then communicate them to the entire staff. They must also agree and commit to "walking the talk." DGI's survey reveals a very clear list of values:

- Ethical/Integrity
- Compassion/Caring
- Balance (Home/Work)
- Client Satisfaction
- Long-Term Perspective/Vision
- Excellence/Continuous Improvement
- Collaboration/Teamwork
- Candor/Honesty/Openness

When asked to rank-order these values, the DGI staff results were as follows:

1. Ethical/Integrity
2. Client Satisfaction
3. Compassion/Caring

FCG believes that this is the "correct" answer for investment firms. The first lens that must be used in decision making must be, "Is it ethical? Does it pass the integrity test?" The second lens is, "Does it serve the client?" (When you get these two reversed, as Andersen did with Enron, it can bankrupt the entire firm.) The third highest ranking value for DGI—Compassion/Caring—is unique in the industry: 70% of DGI's staff chose Compassion/Caring as a core value at the firm, whereas in the industry overall, only 7% of investment professionals choose it as a core value.

In trying to make sense of this third value (Compassion/Caring), it is helpful to know a bit about CEO Martin. The book that is foundational for Fred is the one by Kiel, mentioned earlier. Kiel asserts that there are certain principles that are universal and hold true for people in all cultures everywhere. Through his extensive research, he arrives at four that he claims are "vital for sustained personal and organizational success."[50] You read about them earlier:

- Integrity
- Responsibility
- Compassion
- Forgiveness

When I asked Fred why these are considered principles, he responded, "Because they are like gravity. If you jump out a window, you will fall to the earth. If you violate these principles repeatedly over time, your firm will fall to earth, i.e. implode."[51] So, in Fred's mind these are the core principles that he practices and encourages at DGI. An example: When one of the staff members encountered personal difficulties (illness in the family), Fred encouraged that person to be candid with teammates. (The more typical behavior is to hide such information so as not to appear weak or needy.) The response of the team was overwhelming support to the team member in question. Specifically, they said, "Take all the time you need at home. We've got you covered." Clearly the staff was demonstrating the principle of compassion. Trust was enhanced at the firm when the staff's response was "we've got your back."

Fred went on to explain that good leaders practice the first two principles really well: integrity and responsibility. In his view, though, outstanding leaders practice all four. From the perspective of personality types, Fred is echoing the wisdom of Myers-Briggs theory: that good leaders operate as both "Thinkers" and "Feelers." They integrate the head (**T**) and the heart (**F**) in their leadership. Thinking leaders can become overly focused on tasks and results, leaving the staff overworked and underappreciated. Feeling leaders can be overly concerned with harmony and relationships, resulting in complacency, poor accountability, and inferior work product. (The crayon-simple version of this leadership balance is represented by the leader who must choose between the open hand (compassion/forgiveness) and the closed fist (integrity/responsibility). Try this experiment right now: Open one of your hands, while making a fist with the other. Now alternate between the feeling of the two hands: open and receptive versus firm and deliberate. Those are your basic leadership tools. Knowing when to use each is wisdom.

Let's look at more data from the earlier discussion of firms A and B. I showed the continuum charts for the choices that all firms face: long-term vs. short-term, sales-centric vs. investment-centric, collaborative vs. star-based. In the following charts, note that DGI is remarkably aligned on these choices. Fred has clearly communicated to his senior team and the larger staff where DGI stands on these issues. They are not confused about who they are or how they operate.

In the charts in Table 2.16, the employees at each firm were asked to place their firm on the continuum that we discussed earlier. When FCG reviews the survey results, we look for alignment around one view. In most cases there is not a "correct" view, but rather a range of responses. In average to good companies, employees have a variety of views and are unaligned. In great companies, leaders have discussed and agreed upon their firm's approach and then communicated that approach to the staff. Note the close alignment for the DGI staff.

Table 2.16 Short-Term vs. Long-Term Results

	DGI	Firm A	Firm B
Leaders seem focused on the short-term results	0%	41%	46%
Neutral	41%	20%	22%
Leaders seem focused on the long-term results	59%	39%	32%

Nearly all the DGI staff understand that the firm is run with long-term perspective (which was also seen in their choice of core values: Long-term perspective/Vision is a core value). Now consider the next continuum, the all-important question: Are we more interested in growing AUM or in delivering top performance? Table 2.17 shows how the three firms in question responded to this choice.

Table 2.17 Asset Gathering vs. Investment Performance

	DGI	Firm A	Firm B
Leaders are mostly focused on asset gathering (sales-centric)	9%	46%	52%
Neutral	20%	25%	14%
Leaders are mostly focused on fund performance (investment-centic)	71%	29%	36%

Again, we see that DGI has established great clarity about the firm's mission: first and foremost we take care of the client by providing top performance. (Which they have done!)

The next continuum question explores the question of communication: How transparent are we? Do we share information freely (blue), or do we operate more on a "need to know" basis (gold)? DGI is the most transparent of the three, as Table 2.18 shows.

Table 2.18 Communication Continuum

Transparency vs. Need to know	DGI	Firm A	Firm B
Leaders seem to favor transparency and openness of information	78%	46%	34%
Neutral	15%	22%	31%
Leaders approach information on a "need to know" basis	7%	32%	35%

Another challenge for all investment firms is candor. Are staff members willing to debate and confront one another? (blue) Or do they value harmony and diplomacy more? (gold; see Table 2.19). Here is a place where DGI has shown skillful leadership. Despite their commitment to compassion, which suggests kindness and harmony (read: less candor), they are still willing to challenge each other. I would argue that DGI's candor is the result of high trust and respect levels. Firms A and B have work to do in this area.

Table 2.19 Candor Continuum

Team members: Challenging vs. Polite	DGI	Firm A	Firm B
Team members frequently challenge each other, have open debate	54%	42%	39%
Neutral	31%	15%	22%
Team members are tactful and polite in their discussion, rarely debating	15%	43%	39%

The final comparison involves worker autonomy. In *Drive*, Dan Pink makes a compelling case for flexible work styles: Give staff members the freedom to choose how, where, and when they want to do their work. In FCG's client engagements we see this desire for autonomy in the younger generations especially. Gen Xers and Yers are very interested in work/life balance. Firms that are resistant to this balance run the risk of losing talent. Our last continuum (Table 2.20) asks if a firm's leaders favor face time and rigid schedules (blue) or autonomy: get the results however you wish (gold).

Table 2.20 Autonomy Continuum

Focus: Face time vs. Results only	DGI	Firm A	Firm B
Leaders pay attention to face time, i.e. number of hours in the office	5%	32%	45%
Neutral	11%	24%	15%
Leaders are focused on results only, i.e. employees have complete autonomy as to how they get thier results	84%	44%	40%

Clearly, DGI favors autonomy more than the other two firms. Fred is very aware of the power of autonomy and what it means to have a "virtual office." We discussed in some detail the new technologies for communicating and the role that social media plays in the investment scene today. Despite Fred's chronological age—70—he is young in spirit and respects the different values that younger workers bring to the job.

As evidence that Fred is open to new ideas, consider a recent initiative at the firm called "Project Bold." Here's a description of their project:

> At Disciplined Growth Investors we have a close-knit team that is curious, passionate and a little eccentric. In their own ways, they each exemplify the qualities that make DGI unique. In order to recognize and encourage what our people were already doing, we created Project Bold. DGI sponsors employees as they make bold moves in their own lives. To try something new. To stare down the unknown until it hands over its secrets. To ride no coat tails. To rest on no laurels.

All of the employees were given $2,000 by the firm, with the condition that they had to use the money to stretch themselves, to challenge themselves. Here is the story of one employee.

> Prior to her Bold Initiative, Cindy had never traveled without her husband. Moreover, except for a short trip to Canada, Cindy had never traveled outside the United States. So, a nine-day trip to Costa Rica, alone, was a somewhat novel concept for her.

> Although she was a little anxious, Cindy was able to pull a plan together. She managed every step: passports, booking, airports, taxis, hotels, meals, and activities. From her doorstep in Minnesota to Costa Rica and back, she made it through every step on her own.

While in Costa Rica, Cindy biked trails, rafted the Reventazon River, visited a jaguar refuge, took a bird-watching tour, rode a zipline across a wooded ravine, and trudged through the Manzanillo nature area on a guided hike. "The sights and sounds in Costa Rica are absolutely amazing. My senses were overloaded the entire time I was there."

Although Cindy speaks no Spanish, she was able to rely on the kindness of strangers. "I met a lot of people from around the world. There was a spirit of helpfulness that I didn't realize was out there."

Overall, the experience was very empowering. "Being by myself gave me a whole different perspective. It wasn't something I would have done before, but now I realize it's something I can do."

FCG has high regard for Fred and his team at DGI. If asked to sum up the secrets of their success, we would go back to Fred and his personal commitment to the core principles:

- Integrity
- Responsibility
- Compassion
- Forgiveness

Each of these principles folds into the behaviors of high-performing teams that FCG has written and spoken about over the years. *Integrity* is about making and keeping clear agreements: having your words and actions line up. *Responsibility* is about having a conscience: taking responsibility for your actions, not blaming others or hiding. *Compassion* is about empathy: putting yourself in someone else's place, showing that you care about your fellow workers, establishing connection and a sense of "we're all in this together." *Forgiveness* recognizes that none of us is perfect: we all make mistakes. Can we forgive ourselves and our colleagues and allow for fresh starts? FCG calls this the "drift and shift" model. We drift off our commitments, notice it (or get feedback!), and then recommit to those original commitments.

Firms A and B should take heart: the goal *is* reachable, as DGI has shown. The main ingredient to success is strong leadership and commitment. In our view, that is the secret to DGI's success.

Okay, let's extend this discussion of culture with more detail about the leader's job: to define culture, shape it, practice it, and maintain it. Easy. Right?

13   Dave Ulrich, *The Leadership Capital Index* (Berrett-Koehler, 2015).

14   *360* refers to the fact that feedback is gathered from bosses, peers, and direct reports: hence the visual image of "360 degrees."

15   This is an extreme statement but true: we canvassed the whole firm and found *no one* who supported his leadership abilities.

16   See Michael Lewis, *Liar's Poker* (2004), https://www.pdfdrive.net/liars-poker-by-michael-lewis-i-e31388161.html, for a description of BSDs (Big Swinging D—ks).

17   I wish I could be gender-neutral in my criticism of investment leaders, but, alas, the senior positions are mostly held by men.

18   I love my 95-year-old mom's recent comment about mirrors: "Their quality has really gone down in the last few years."

19   See Margaret Heffernan's excellent book, *Willful Blindness* (Bloomsbury, 2012).

20   Andrew Lo, "The Gordon Gekko Effect: The Role of Culture in the Financial Industry," *Economic Policy Review 22* (1)(January 4, 2016), https://www.newyorkfed.org/medialibrary/media/research/epr/2016/epr_2016_gordon-gekko-effect_lo.pdf?la=en. Special thanks to Tom Brakke for bringing my attention to this paper. Lo opens the paper by stating: "Culture is a potent force in shaping individual and group behavior, yet it has received scant attention … ." I couldn't help it: At gunpoint, my ego made me send Andy an email indicating the FCG has produced 3 books, 15 white papers, 37 blogs, and more than 200 speeches on the topic … but who's counting?

21   Zimbardo asked Stanford students to participate in an experiment where some students were prison guards and others were prisoners. Within a few days, the experiment devolved into "Lord of the Flies" behavior and Zimbardo had to end the experiment early.

22   Lo, "The Gordon Gekko Effect," p. 34.

23   FCG, "The Investment Challenge" (2015), p. 8; http://www.focuscgroup.com/wp-content/uploads/2015/11/The_Investment_Challenge.pdf

24   Kudos to my partners Keith and Michael, as they frequently will call BS on clients when appropriate. Michael by nature has a healthy dose of conscience, courage, and skepticism, which makes him an excellent whistleblower.

25   Better yet, form what Eisenhower called a "kitchen cabinet," composed of people who will speak the truth to you in private. I adopted that idea years ago from Fred Martin, CEO of Disciplined Growth Investors.

26   See the paper we co-authored with Jason Hsu, "The Folly of Blame," *Journal of Portfolio Management* 41(3): 23 34; http://www.focuscgroup.com/wp-content/uploads/2015/11/Folly-of-Blame-JPM.pdf

27   This rule has been mentioned throughout the series, but it wasn't given a specific number until season 7, episode 12: "Flesh and Blood". The rule is also a direct reference to John Wayne's catchphrase in *She Wore a Yellow Ribbon* (John Ford, director). Wayne said: "Never apologize, mister, it's a sign of weakness" to subordinates in a military situation. DiNozzo notes the connection in season 3, episode 23, "Hiatus Part 1." Mark Harmon's career has paralleled John Wayne's. They both were quarterback of their southern California college football team, both went into acting. (Harmon's father, Tom Harmon, was a Heisman Trophy winner and actor/announcer as well.) Note: This is continuously told to Tony, Ziva, and Tim through a smack to the back of their heads.

28   Fred Martin, quoted earlier, is one of my whistleblowers. In reviewing this blog/paper, he added these good thoughts: "Please be specific about your own kitchen cabinet. You were too cavalier about your wife's influences. I was left wondering what kinds of specific decisions she helped you with. You also should be more specific about your associates. What specifically have they done to help you deal with your blindspots? Are there any other members of your kitchen cabinet?" *JW: Fred makes a good point. I think the response is long enough to constitute another LOL blog posting—which I intend to do.*

29   Fred Kiel, *Return on Character: The Real Reason Leaders and Their Companies Win* (Harvard Business Review Press, 2015).

30   Doug Lennick and Fred Kiel, *Moral Intelligence* (Pearson Prentice Hall, 2005).

31   Kiel, *Return on Character*, p. 3.

32   Ulrich, *The Leadership Capital Index*, p. 57.

33   See our website and white papers on the Focus Elite firms. They are not a secret. We write and speak about them frequently.

34   Kiel, *Return on Character*, p. 34.

35   Gervase Bushe, *Clear Leadership: Sustaining Real Collaboration and Partnership at Work* (Nicholas Brealey, 2010).

36   *Ibid.*

37   *Ibid.*

38   Bushe, *Clear Leadership*, p. 35.

39   *Ibid.*, p. 58.

40   *Ibid.*, p. 79.

41   *Ibid.*, p. 34.

42   *Ibid.*, p. 111.

43   *Ibid.*, p. 145.

44   Focus Consulting Group, "The Investment Challenge" (2015), http://www.focuscgroup.com/wp-content/uploads/2015/11/The_Investment_Challenge.pdf.

45   All of these books are available on Amazon.

46   Pink, *Drive*.

47   See Appendix H for more on this topic.

48   Pink, *Drive*.

49   Cali Ressler and Jody Thompson, *Why Work Sucks and How to Fix It* (Portfolio, 2010).

50   Kiel, *Return on Character*, p. 45.

51   Interview with Fred Martin, June 13, 2015.

CHAPTER 3

Culture: Code of Conduct

nvestment culture has become accepted as a key ingredient of success. In surveys around the world, 97% of investment professionals agree with the statement: "Culture is important to our firm's success."[52] When asked the logical follow-up question—Why? What are the benefits?—two answers repeatedly stand out: 1) talent (attracting and retaining) and 2) decision making. These answers make sense: investment professionals want to work at reputable shops that have strong investment cultures and good decision making. We summarize the benefits of culture in the word *workability*. In other words, strong culture means an environment which supports good work. There are minimum distractions and red tape. Professionalism reigns, drama is minimized.

The core of such a culture consists of three factors:

1. *Purpose:* a clear and compelling reason for existing. Meaningful work. Belonging to something that is bigger than oneself. Chapter 1 covered this topic.
2. *Trust:* sufficient levels of trust in one's leaders and colleagues. More on this topic in Chapter 4.
3. *Values:* a set of values and behaviors that are unique to investment work.

Purpose

Chapter 1 covered purpose pretty thoroughly, so there's not much more to add here. Purpose aligns and motivates staff. Increasingly, leaders are becoming aware of this reality. FCG regularly gets calls from firms inquiring about purpose: "How can we create a compelling statement of purpose?" The response to this question involves thinking in bigger terms than your day-to-day operations. Often the word *legacy* helps leaders to open their thinking: "What lasting impact do I want to leave?" In any case, culture suffers when the firm's purpose is mundane.

Trust

Trust is the platform on which workability operates. Trust is a skill. When professionals understand the components of it, they can commit to becoming increasingly trustworthy. The six factors that influence trust are:

1. Interests aligned (common goals and incentives)
2. Benevolent concern (win/win, we care about each other)
3. Capabilities (competence, ability to deliver promised results)
4. Predictability and integrity (consistency, reliability over time, words and actions aligning)
5. Frequent and open communication (transparency)
6. Vulnerability (willingness to own your errors, apologize, and admit when you don't know something)

When teams have trust issues, it's useful to trot out these factors and ask, "Which ones are deficient? That is, which are leading to the distrust?" Sometimes a firm's compensation system pits colleagues against each other. Sometimes a person is in the wrong role, so his colleagues think, "He's a good guy, but he's *not* good in that role … so, I don't trust his work product." Still other times, a colleague is inconsistent. She is usually trustworthy, but occasionally there are significant lapses. If sufficient openness and candor exist for a team, then honest discussions can help identify and clear up the trust issues. More on this important topic in Chapter 4.

Values

Values come in two varieties. There are the traditional values that constitute the DNA of the industry, and then there are the unique values that allow a particular firm to excel. The traditional ones are:

1. Client satisfaction
2. Ethics/integrity
3. Teamwork
4. Excellence

Regardless of where a firm operates or what products it offers, these basic "DNA strands" are common to all divisions in all investment firms. Or should be. (The CFA Institute has been a strong advocate of the first two in its mission.)

Over and above these core values, each major "tribe" in the investment firm—(1) research and portfolio management; (2) sales, marketing, and client facing; and (3) support functions, like operations, IT, legal, financial, compliance, etc.—has a unique set of additional values that fit with their role in the firm. Research shows that the additional values are as shown in Table 3.1.

Table 3.1 Additional "Tribal" Values

Tribes within the Investment Firm	Additional Values (Satellite)
Research and portfolio management (and trading)	Analytic/Research, Disciplined, Creativity/Innovation, Meritocracy
Support functions	Accountability, Efficiency, Quality/Precision
Sales, marketing, client facing	Competitive/Win, Passion/Energy/Positive, Humor/Fun

Investment cultures can start to fray when the natural tensions that exist between the subcultures flare up. For example, every investment leader has seen times when compliance and marketing butt heads. The value of identifying the core values is that they represent common ground. If two tribes are squabbling, a skillful leader will remind them of the "meta-values" (such as client service or teamwork) to help get them back in alignment.

Of particular interest, then, is the set of values that a firm has developed over and above these core and satellite values in the industry. What values, behaviors, or attitudes will allow for even greater workability? Are there ground rules or principles that, if practiced, would promote greater success? An example of a firm that has taken this approach to the extreme is Bridgewater Capital in the United States. Founder Ray Dalio wrote out his principles in a document—and later a book—titled *Principles for Success—*.[53] There are more than 200 tips for better teamwork and decision making in this document. A big believer in candor, Dalio writes, "If you think it, say it." One of many radical practices at Bridgewater is recording all meetings so that there is a public record as to what was said and decided. In this way, Bridgewater takes seriously the difference between "fact" and "story." If an employee claims that he did not support a certain decision, there is a way to determine if that is a fact! Other firms have come up with these ground rules for improved performance:

- Outlaw any handheld devices in the meeting room, so that people stay focused on the discussion.
- Lock the door to the meeting room when the "start" time arrives, so that people learn to be on time.
- Use precise cultural language such as "fact" and "story" to differentiate between a fact and someone's opinion. The rule of thumb for determining a fact is that everyone present must agree to it.
- Clear up trust issues within 24 hours of the incident (this is called the "24-hour rule").
- Designate a period of hours during the day when no interruptions are allowed. Each person is guaranteed quiet time to think deeply about work issues. (Some of you may begin drooling when you read that one! Sounds great, doesn't it?!)
- Use email only for information, *not* for settling emotional issues.
- Allow people to manage their own work schedules: they can work anywhere, anytime, and in any way they choose, as long as the work gets done.
- For all meetings, designate a "devil's advocate" who is charged with disagreeing with and challenging prevailing ideas. Rotate the role so that one person doesn't get labeled as cantankerous.

Firms that are responding well and competing effectively to the ever-more-challenging investment conditions have thought carefully about the culture that best supports their mission. They have culture by design, not default.

The key to developing and sustaining strong culture is vigilance. Strong culture, like a beautiful garden, must be weeded, watered, and cared for. Leaders must understand that it is part of their job to set the example and to constantly be appreciating workers who model good behavior. Too many leaders are excellent at pointing out flaws but *not* at rewarding the positive. Research on this aspect of culture is clear: appreciation is far more powerful as a motivator than criticism. Yes, you must give critical feedback when appropriate, but learn to spot and reward the right behaviors. Most importantly, the senior team must walk the talk—and when they don't, they must have the courage and integrity to provide feedback to one another. Strong culture will provide a winning edge for the firm, but like anything of great value, it does not come without effort.

Respect as a fundamental value

On our culture journey I've indicated that several values are important to building a strong and enduring culture of workability. For example, there are the four elements that we see repeatedly in the investment world:

1. Clients
2. Integrity
3. Teamwork
4. Excellence

Then there is the all-important value of trust, which every leader acknowledges as top priority. Finally, there are the values that Kiel endorses in his book:

- Integrity
- Responsibility (Accountability)
- Compassion
- Forgiveness

No question, these are important to leadership and strong culture. But there is another value—or perhaps *behavior* is a better term—that is so basic it gets overlooked: Respect.

Of course, CEOs endorse respect as fundamental to a great workplace, and FCG agrees. Respect is key to strong culture and good performance. In fact, when we ask investment staff members to select the antidotes to bad behaviors (what FCG calls "sludge") in their firm's culture, we get these results consistently (Table 3.2).

Table 3.2 Sludge-Reduction Behaviors

Which behaviors/attitudes below would help to reduce this firm's sludge? (pick 3)	
More trust	25%
More respect	21%
More accountability	18%
More clarity	15%
All other choices	21%

More trust and more respect will reduce bad behaviors. We'll cover trust shortly, but here I focus on respect.

Despite paying lip-service to respect, many firms experience a big "say-do" gap. That is, they say one thing ("we deeply believe in respect") and they do another ("disrespect is okay if you are a big enough contributor"). For many firms, a more accurate culture statement would be: Our first priority is making money, after which we'd like our people to be respectful. An example: A CEO spoke at length about the importance of respect at a meeting and, immediately afterward, publicly chewed out his PA for a minor mistake in scheduling. When I asked him about it privately, he rolled his eyes at me and said, "C'mon, I've got a business to run." That's the "say-do" gap at its finest.

Let's examine respect a little more carefully. To be clear, there is a difference between respecting someone and showing respect for someone. The former suggests a genuine high regard for someone's character or work product. The latter is simply a choice that we all make to treat someone with respect, regardless of their abilities or performance. Before articulating this difference, we asked a roomful of investment professionals to respond to the statement in Table 3.3.

Table 3.3 Degrees of Respect

It is ok to treat people at work with different degrees of respect	
Agree	45%
Neutral	0%
Disagree	55%

As you can see from the results, nearly half the room felt that it was okay to treat people with different degrees of respect. We discussed this voting outcome for a moment, and some of the participants got animated about it. "Really!? You think it is okay to treat people with less respect?" When we unpacked the meaning behind people's votes, it became clear that some voters were saying, "I have different levels of respect for co-workers"(a reasonable statement), whereas others were saying, "Regardless what level of respect I have for them, I will treat them with respect." When we defined the word *respect* more precisely, we voted again, with the result in Table 3.4.

Table 3.4 Revised Respect Question

Respect is a choice. I commit to treating all of my colleagues with dignity and respect	
Agree	100%
Neutral	0%
Disagree	0%

All participants agreed: regardless of how much I respect someone, I should treat everyone with respect. This distinction is important because many people operate from the view that "if I don't respect them, then I don't have to treat them with respect." However, as we see in the votes in Table 3.4, when the distinction is examined and made clear, all the participants agree: even when you don't fully respect someone, it is still important to *treat* them respectfully.

Often old-fashioned mindsets still govern the core structures and processes of firms: specifically, the way that leaders think about face time or the way they handle compensation and succession issues. If your firm truly endorses respect as a fundamental value, then it is worth considering new approaches.

For example, in FCG's view the whole mindset of face time is disrespectful. It implies that workers can't be trusted to be productive on their own. They must be at their desks to get "credit" for being productive. Scott Adams is aware of the face time dilemma:

Many good firms still are anchored in a face time mindset. An example is given in Table 3.5.

Table 3.5 Face Time vs. Results Only

Leaders pay attention to facetime, i.e. number of hours in the office	**70%**
Neutral	**18%**
Leaders are focused on results only, i.e. employees have complete autonomy as to how they get their results	**12%**

The firm that produced these results has a great culture and great performance in the markets, but still retains a strong emphasis on face time. FCG views this as a disconnect. If you really trust and respect your staff, you will *not* value face time. Instead, you will move to a results-only work environment, in which you trust people to get their work done in whatever fashion they choose. My point here is that if one of your firm's chosen values is respect, then why aren't you practicing it by eliminating mandatory face time? The answer for many firms is "We've always done it that way." In other words, we've always respected people who get in early and work long hours. Fine. But in the modern workforce, most staff members can work long hours from anywhere! If you trust and respect your staff, you'll shift the mindset from "work is a place you go" to "work is something you do." Face time will evaporate as a measure of productivity. Both leaders and workers will focus on what really matters: results.

Another practice that often promotes disrespect in the workplace is compensation. The traditional approach to comp design and execution is to collect industry data from the well-established vendors, study it behind closed doors, then decide and announce what is "fair" to the workers. Occasionally this process works. Far too often, the workers feel—you guessed it—disrespected because they were not part of the process. In FCG's view, the respectful way to design a comp package is to involve the staff members in the discussion. When FCG explained this approach to one CEO, he instinctively responded, "Whoa! That means you're letting the inmates run the asylum." We waited a moment, and this CEO—a normally wise and compassionate person—smiled and said, "I can't believe I just said that." Well, he did, and many CEOs have the same knee-jerk reaction: "We have to retain control of comp. Heaven forbid we'd include the staff members in the discussion!" Rest assured, if you include the staff members, the process works better, not worse. They feel respected and are much more likely to buy into the outcome when they've been consulted.

Yet another practice that promotes disrespect is succession. As with compensation, many firms discuss and decide key promotions at the senior level behind closed doors, with very little input and very little transparency. FCG has had great success in using a completely different model, in which all the relevant staff members are included in the design of the position in question. For example, if the firm's CIO is nearing retirement (which could mean three years in advance), then the firm's CEO would begin the discussion of the job description for the next CIO. Often, the nature of the position has changed due to markets, products, maturity of the firm, and so on. So, the old adage, "What got you here won't get you there" becomes relevant. When FCG facilitates these succession discussions, we ask all the investment staff members to debate and weigh in on which competencies will be most important in the future. Perhaps the retiring CIO was mostly an internal figure—championing the investment philosophy and process—whereas the new CIO must be much more an external figure, excellent at selling and marketing the delivery of investment outcomes. By including the investment staff in the design of the new role, you show them a high level of respect. Also, judging by FCG's experience, you get a much better picture of the competencies required of the new CIO. Wins for everyone involved.

The common denominator of all these suggested improvements is "treat adults like adults." It's good to remember that people live up—or down—to the expectations placed on them.[54] If you treat people like adults, you'll be surprised: they act like adults! So, whether the issue is work schedules, compensation, succession, or something else, assume that your staff members are adults and treat them that way. They will feel respected, and the firm will get better results.

No advice on respect would be complete without one simple reminder: "Practice good listening." People identify listening as the number-one ingredient to feeling respected. Giving people your undivided attention is one sure way to show respect. It's not always easy in our hyperactive, multitasking world! Put away your device and *listen*.

Leadership and Culture Change

Finally, the ultimate question: How does a leader change culture, or to use different words, how does a leader influence/shape culture?

How do you manage culture change? We saw earlier that 97% of investment professionals agree that "Strong culture contributes to success." According to our clients, strong culture attracts talent, improves morale, enhances decision making, and increases client satisfaction. So, how do you manage it to get these benefits?

For many years, FCG has effectively used a model we call ESAR. The elements of ESAR are shown in Figure 3.1.

Figure 3.1 Managing Culture: E-S-A-R

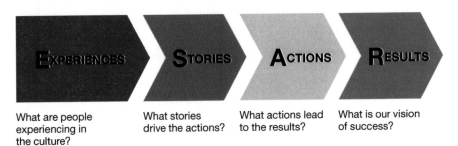

| What are people experiencing in the culture? | What stories drive the actions? | What actions lead to the results? | What is our vision of success? |

The model starts with the basic questions: What are we trying to achieve? What are the firm's goals? What results will satisfy our stakeholders (i.e., clients, employees, and owners)? Culture exists to support the firm's goals, so without the end in mind, culture efforts are misguided.

For our purposes, we'll assume that leadership has done its work and that vision, mission, and strategy are in place.

Here's how ESAR works. The three key pieces are:

1. **Experiences:** What do people experience in their everyday work life? These statements would be largely factual, such as, "I hear team members grumbling about lack of candor in meetings." Another example might be: "I've never heard leaders explain how the bonus system works at this firm."
2. **Stories:** How do people interpret their daily experiences? What stories are created to explain the experiences? In the example concerning candor from #1 in this list, people might create various stories:
   a. The leader has intimidated team members so that they are afraid to participate … or
   b. The team is bored with the topics, they don't participate because they have no interest … or
   c. The team is ill-informed so they can't contribute intelligently.
   As humans, we naturally interpret our experiences. Nature abhors a vacuum and so do our minds. We fill gaps with our own interpretations, right or wrong.

3. **Actions:** The stories that are created will drive our actions. For example, if the people in the meeting feel that they will be punished for speaking freely, then they will be silent.

Managing culture becomes an exercise in understanding how the experiences and stories in your firm are driving actions (i.e., behavior). Feedback is an important tool because often leaders will not know what stories are circulating unless they receive real-time information. For example, during an offsite a participant said, "One of the reasons why so many of us are nervous is because we have heard rumors that our new CEO is here to sell the business." The CEO—who was in the room—was shocked by this statement. The CEO's response was an unequivocal "No, that is not why I was brought in." In relatively short order, that inaccurate story was cleared up, and the tension dissipated.

The job for leaders and all staff members is one of listening for predominant stories: knowing the "buzz." Then they must reinforce the good stories—the ones that drive good results—and address the bad ones that hurt morale and performance.

A common "bad" story held by staff members is that the boss does *not* want to be challenged. Sometimes, of course, the story is true. Some bosses do punish team members for pushing back on ideas. If that is the case, then the experience created by the boss has to change. The ESAR model is pointing to the "experience," rather than the "story," as the source of the problem.

In contrast, we have often found that the story is inaccurate. Actually, the boss does want pushback but has given contradictory signals. She may roll her eyes or make a sarcastic comment when someone offers a different view. An effective way to correct this inaccurate story is for the boss to address it directly: "I do want to hear your views, even when they differ from mine. Please test me on this." Then, as a skillful follow-up, the boss can begin by asking, "Does anyone see this point differently?" Most importantly, the boss must align words and actions. When a different view is expressed, the boss must show clearly that she welcomes it. In the beginning, it is useful to make this point forcefully by mentioning later in the meeting that you appreciate so-and-so for his earlier pushback. In this way, the boss can correct the bad story and improve the dynamics of the team.

Culture change occurs when enough leaders and staff members understand and employ the ESAR model. Underlying all culture change is the mindset of the firm. *Mindset* is the beliefs, opinions, expectations, and assumptions that are operative in a firm (i.e., "stories" in FCG language). The tricky part is that they are unseen. It is relatively easy to correct culture violations that are seen, like coming late to meetings. It is much harder to address the ones that are invisible, like distrusting your colleagues.

For example, the issue of distrust arose on one team because the leader was often absent, leading to a story that he was selfish and detached from the team's success. The experience in this case was accurate: The leader was frequently away, and when the leader was present, he seemed uninterested in the team's work. The stories created by the team hurt morale and productivity. FCG was asked to work with the situation and see if we could improve it. In interviewing the leader, we learned rather quickly that his wife had been diagnosed with cancer. They had three young children. The leader was in crisis. Rather than share this information with his team, he chose to keep it to himself. When the interview was ending, we asked if he would be willing to share the news with his team. At first, he didn't see the point: It was a private matter, not involving work. We explained that in fact the situation was a work matter because he was taking time off and becoming detached from his duties. Rather reluctantly, this leader agreed to share his situation with his team. As you can imagine, this information had a profound effect on them. The story that he was untrustworthy evaporated and the team showed both genuine concern for him and a willingness to help in any way they could. By addressing the inaccurate story, the leader resolved the situation. (There is a happy ending to this tale: His wife has since recovered and remained in remission.)

Not all ESAR stories are this dramatic or so fully resolved. Nevertheless, the ESAR model is the core tool for addressing mindsets and behavior in a firm. The best way to practice ESAR is to take situations at work and break them down into the three basic components: experiences, stories, and actions. For example, say you overhear two colleagues gossiping that so-and-so got a poor job review because they saw him leave the HR director's office with an angry expression, muttering to himself. You can break down this situation as follows:

1. **Experience:** So-and-so was seen leaving the HR director's office.
2. **Story:** He was angry because he got a bad job review.
3. **Action:** Two colleagues gossip about the event.

If your culture is built on trust and respect, such an action should be discouraged, because gossip tends to erode trust. So-and-so would not be pleased with two colleagues spreading a story that he got a bad review—whether it's true or not.

Too many leaders are passive around the experiences and stories that live in their firm. Actions and results are visible and therefore more easily addressed. However, leaders who are unaware of—or unconcerned about—the underlying cause of the actions will not address the core issues. Learning the ESAR model and using it to address the real issues is the proven approach for strengthening culture.

The ESAR model describes a good process for addressing culture change, but a sizeable number of misunderstandings about culture and behavior change remains. Staff members look at a list of core values—things like integrity, respect, trust, and so on—and think, "Yes, it would be nice if *others* did these things." There are two major problems with this reaction:

1. It overlooks the obvious fact that you only have control over yourself. So, expecting others to change is not useful. But it's what most people do. (*If my spouse would just change …*)
2. If everyone adopts this way of thinking—that others should change—then no one has accepted responsibility for changing their *own* behavior. They are waiting for others to get with the program. Thus, nothing changes.

The simple truth is that *no one* in your firm has perfect integrity, or shows perfect respect, or is completely trustworthy. Including you. So, look in the mirror and do an honest assessment regarding your behavior. Here are the key mental shifts that each of us must understand if we are serious about changing our behavior to improve culture:

1. **A genuine desire to take the values seriously and commit to them.** Here's the catch. Most people agree with the value of wellness/good health. But how many exercise regularly and eat healthy? (Hint: Go to the mall and look around to see the answer.) Living the values of your firm requires the same discipline and vigilance as staying in good shape.
2. **A realistic WIIFM.** Given that aligning and living the values requires work, you must ask yourself honestly, "What's in it for me?" (WIIFM). Some people are very principled and will live the values because it's right. Others want to fit in and be accepted, so they'll conform due to social standards. Still others see that being a good corporate citizen is the path to success and promotions. For me personally, I just feel better when I live in accordance with my values and those of our firm. (My personal values are wisdom and compassion. FCG's are curiosity, accountability, candor, and appreciation—"caca" for short …)

3. **A significant amount of humility.** You must accept the premise that you could improve your behavior regarding any of the values. No one is perfect. Most of us aren't even *nearly* perfect. Don't kid yourself. Where are you weak?

4. **An openness to feedback.** You will not improve if you have walled yourself off. I coach leaders who tell me that they show respect to all their team members. (When challenged, they say indignantly: "Of course I do!") But when I interview the team members they say, "No, he is very disrespectful at times." The problem is that some leaders have sufficiently intimidated the team members that no one provides candid feedback. No one keeps the leader honest. (All leaders should have such a person.) You won't see your blindspots if no one points them out. Eyes wide open, please.

5. **A healthy dose of vulnerability.** Because we all take two steps forward and one step back on the values journey, we must learn to make amends. Put a little sign on your mirror, "I will screw up, so I will make amends." Because it *will* happen. How do I know? Because we are all human. Get past your Ego telling you not to apologize—because it's weak or embarrassing or unprofessional—and learn to do it as soon as you realize that you've violated a value. (When you snipe at a colleague—"some of us get our work done on time"—clean it up right after the meeting. A simple, "Sorry, I shouldn't have taken that shot at you" will do.)

6. **A realistic attitude.** Lose your perfectionism. As stated previously, behavior change is *not* about being perfect. It's about gradual progress in the right direction. Progress is a strong motivator. Your mantra: *Progress over Perfection*. (You can put that on your mirror, too.)

7. **A habit of appreciation.** When you or a colleague do make a bit of progress, appreciate yourself or them. The investment industry is horrible at this simple practice. (We call it ADD: Appreciation Deficit Disorder.) People need to be appreciated and recognized for their progress. Usually, though, instead of looking for what colleagues do right—their progress—we focus on their mistakes. Shift from fault-finding to success-spotting. When I hear staff members say, "So-and-so was making progress during his coaching, but now he's fallen back to his old behavior," I ask, "Have you given him encouragement? Have you success-spotted?" Invariably the answer is no. Cause and effect. Reinforcement matters.

8. **A willingness to forgive.** Because no one in the firm will do behavior change perfectly, you must develop an ability to forgive. It's important to give your colleagues the benefit of the doubt and assume good intentions. Personally, I tell myself frequently, "People are doing the best they can." Remember, no one wakes up and sets an intention to break as many cultural norms as possible at work. Instead of negatively judging your colleague and holding tightly to your story, forgive them. Then have the courage to provide useful feedback.

9. **An understanding of "drift and shift."** You will drift off your commitment to live the values, so recognize when you have, and then—instead of chastising yourself—just recommit. You drift off your commitment, then shift back to it. Punishing yourself (or others) doesn't help, but feedback does.

All of these mental shifts point back to #1: Have you considered the values and made a serious commitment to them? When we do real-time voting with staff members, we invariably get a unanimous—or nearly unanimous—response to the question, "Are you committed to the firm's values?" However, the follow-up behavior doesn't align with this response. Many people do not change at all, even if they accept the premise that we all could do better. A common excuse for not changing is: "Well, the leaders are not following the values, so why should I?" This response relies on the logic that "the leaders are taking the low road, so I will too." How does that response improve your life? Better to ignore what the leaders are doing (although providing feedback is useful) and focus on yourself. Don't you want to be more respectful, more trustworthy, more accountable? Doesn't that improve the quality of your life? And your value as an employee? (Note: If leadership behavior is truly toxic, then you may be facing a career decision. But most leaders we work with are not toxic, merely unconscious about their behavior.) Part of FCG's role is to provide coaching and feedback to leaders who mean well but aren't getting constructive feedback. We'll focus on helping the leaders, while you focus on yourself!

In summary, culture change depends on behavior change. Behavior change requires a deep commitment to the mental shifts outlined previously. The two main levers that you can pull are:

1. A clear understanding that your number-one goal is changing yourself, not your colleagues.
2. A willingness to help your colleagues with step #1 by providing useful feedback and encouragement. You can't change them, but you can improve the odds that they will succeed in changing themselves.

A final word: Even from a purely selfish perspective, the values journey described in this chapter pays huge dividends. I become a better spouse, father, leader, teammate, and friend as I progress on this journey. Yes, it takes work, but it's well worth it. Here's wishing you every success on your journey!

Here I've been talking a lot about trust and using the topic a bit like talk-show hosts who promise: "Stay tuned; we've got [insert megastar guest name] coming up later in the show!" Well, it's time to bring out our featured guest: *trust*.

---

52 Research from FCG's surveys conducted in 10 countries with more than 5,000 investment professionals.

53 Ray Dalio, *Principles for Success*, www.bridgewater.com or https://www.principles.com/.

54 For the best documentary on expectations, watch Alan Porter, "Eye of the Storm" (2012)

CHAPTER 4

Trust: The Platform for Performance

Y ou're in the kitchen preparing dinner and a grease fire erupts on the stove. What do you do?

A. Remain calm, find a note pad, write down, "To Do's: put out kitchen fire."
B. Ignore it and continue chopping onions. (Remember men: don't cry...)
C. Look disgusted and point a finger at the nearest person, saying, "It's their fault" (my personal favorite ...).
D. Jump into action, alert everyone, put out the fire! (Helpful note: *not* with water.)

Too many teams deal with trust issues as in A, B, or C. Big mistake. Trust is core to team effectiveness. If trust is damaged, team performance will decline (see the overwhelming evidence in this chapter). For this reason, we suggest that you treat trust issues as you would a kitchen fire: In other words, answer D—Jump into action and put it out immediately. You know that any delay could mean a larger fire and possibly injury and severe damage to your home.

Unfortunately, too many teams ignore trust fires. They rationalize that things will get better over time. Time heals all wounds, right? *Wrong*. FCG has seen this mistake time and again. We worked with a senior team that wanted us to deliver a training seminar on trust with their managing directors. While planning this work, we asked, "How is trust at the senior level? That is, with YOU guys." The response was an embarrassed silence and awkward glances. FCG suggested that any serious training in trust must start at the top. The response was, "We tried that, but it didn't go so well." No action was taken.

Within a month of that discussion, the CEO had jumped to another firm. Chalk up another point for "lousy succession." In the weeks that followed, several talented professionals also left the firm, and the exodus continued after that. Morale sank.

We have countless stories like this—and they all hinge on broken trust at the senior level.

Where is the hard evidence that trust matters? FCG performs Team Scorecards on intact investment teams. These scorecards include 24 well-researched factors that lead to team success. Given the nature of the questions and the quantity of data (lots), these Scorecards give us useful insights about trust, candor, debate, and many other factors, including success (defined as "achieving results"). The five factors shown in Table 4.1 are highly correlated with trust.

Table 4.1 Trust Factors

Factor Statement	Correlation
I experience a high level of **candor** and openness on our team.	.88
Conflict is addressed and resolved in a constructive way; we know how to "deal with it" and move on.	.83
We have **common values** and norms that promote good teamwork.	.83
We have a strong sense of **team spirit**; we feel a sense of connection.	.82
We have open and **productive debates**.	.75

For starters, all teams want more candor. They want frank discussions, lively exchanges, open kimonos. Is there a correlation between trust and candor? The data (from 29 teams that filled out our Scorecard) shout "Yes!" to the tune of a correlation coefficient of .88. For these same teams, the mean score for trust (on a 1 to 7 Likert scale, with 7 = strongly agree) is 5.40, and the average for candor is 4.80. Here's the clincher: no team scored higher on candor than on trust. None. In every case, the teams are saying, "We will not achieve high candor without high trust." Trust puts a ceiling on candor. Let me say that again: *Trust puts a ceiling on candor.*

How about conflict resolution? Another frequent request of team leaders is, "Help us resolve tension on the team." Conflict and team spirit are correlated (.80). That makes sense: the more conflict, the lower the team morale. So, does trust correlate with conflict? Indeed it does: .83. And the clincher again: no team scored "resolve conflict" higher than "high level of trust." Trust also puts a ceiling on conflict resolution.

If you are thinking, "Well, trust probably correlates with everything on a team!" Not so. There are team factors that are not heavily dependent on high trust. These factors appear largely unrelated (Table 4.2).

Table 4.2 Factors Unrelated to Trust

Factor Statement	Correlation
I have **clear performance goals** that measure my success on the team.	.30
My work allows me to use my **talents and abilities**.	.29
I know my **role** on the team and what is expected of me.	.24
I feel that my **work is important** to reaching our firm's goals.	.09
I have the **resources** I need to perform my work well.	.06

These results make intuitive sense. The first two factors—goals and roles—are more about clarity. Has the leader articulated them clearly? Leaders can achieve these ends without building high trust on the team. The next two factors seem more individually driven. A team member could be in a role that allows her to use her talents and contribute strongly, without experiencing a high level of trust on the team. Finally, budget constraints might limit resources but not damage trust. Or so the data suggest.

Four teams in the database are "Focus Elite" firms. As noted earlier, these firms demonstrate strong leadership, strong culture, and good success.[55] If we ask how their ratings on the factors "trust" and "success" compare to those of the other firms in the database, we can construct Table 4.3.

Table 4.3 "Trust" and "Success" Correlations

Team	Trust Factor (mean)	Success Factor (mean)
Focus Elite (4 firms)	6.6	5.9
Other firms (25 firms)	5.2	4.9

The headline here is rather obvious: *Trust matters*. A lot.

So, back to the kitchen fire and damaged trust. The antidote is immediate corrective action. Again, put the fire out as soon as you spot it. **Trust Issues = Kitchen Fires**. Burn that one into your memory, the same way that kids learn **Stop, Drop, and Roll**.

So, what are the signs that a Trust Fire has started? John Gottman, a world-renowned expert on trust and relationships, has studied them extensively and come up with what he calls the Four Horsemen of the Apocalypse.[56] Table 4.4 sets out the signs of a Trust Fire and the remedies for each.

Table 4.4 Trust Fire Signs and Remedies

Apocalypse Level	Symptoms	Remedies
1) Defensiveness	Feeling a bit on guard around the other person. Having a story that it is not safe to be open and honest with this person.	Take responsibility. Get curious. What can I learn from this? Notice the stories you make up and practice letting them go. Or test them: Are they accurate?
2) Criticism	Gossiping about the person. Saying to co-workers that the person has weak or bad character, with the intent of making that person wrong. Using absolutes such as: "He always" and "She never".	Notice that you are gossiping and *stop it*. Tell your co-workers, "Stop me if I start to speak ill of a colleague." Think about taking action to fix the trust issue.
3) Stonewalling	Withdrawing from the relationship as a way to avoid conflict. Appearing neutral but actually disapproving and showing stony silence, avoiding the other person.	Notice that you have pulled away altogether and are avoiding the person. Ask yourself: Why are you unwilling to address the issue? Talk to co-workers who do *not* have a trust issue with the person in question.
4) Contempt	Fixed opinion that the other person is fundamentally flawed. He is untrustworthy and there is no point in trying to fix the issue because it won't work.	As for the other elements, check with others who don't see the person as untrustworthy. Assume good intent on the other person's part. Ask a skilled third party to mediate a "clearing" session to see if the trust gap can be fixed.

Gottman has shown that the four levels of distrust are predictable in relationships that are heading south. So, just as the kitchen fire will predictably spread and cause great damage, so will the trust fire. Don't make the mistake of assuming that things will "just get better." Unfortunately, it almost surely goes the other way. The two parties begin to amplify their stories, showing that they are right and the other party is wrong. (Remember our friend Ego? He loves to be right.) They lose sight of the bigger victory—team trust—and go for the petty battle: *I'm right and you are wrong* (sometimes followed by, *"Nyah, nyah, nah, nyah, nyah"*).

The phrase "an ounce of prevention is worth a pound of intervention" is wise counsel. When you feel the slightest trust issue emerge, jump on it immediately. See the kitchen fire in your mind's eye and act. It helps if the whole senior team is familiar with this language and imagery, so that any person can invoke the "kitchen fire" rule—preferably within 24 hours of the incident.

If you don't, these problems tend to worsen. Think of trust issues more like cancer than the common cold. The former requires treatment, the latter gets better on its own. Remember John Gottman's predictable decline: defensiveness, criticism, stonewalling, contempt.

What's the prescription for repair? Remember "Stop, Drop, and Roll?" Well, for trust issues, it's a little more complicated, but FCG has designed a Trust Repair Kit that will help.

Trust Repair Kit

1. Step 1 is to understand the main factors that build or destroy trust. They are listed in Table 4.5 and are pretty self-explanatory.[57] Nothing tricky here.

Table 4.5 Measuring Trust: Key Elements

Trust Factor	Description
Alignment	Do we share the same purpose and goals?
Caring	Do team members care about others or just themselves?
Competency	Do team members produce quality results?
Integrity	Do team members do the "right thing" in a consistent fashion? Do they amke and clear agreements?
Transparency	Do team members communicate openly and honestly? Do they share information? Do they avoid secrecy and hidden agendas?
Vulnerability	Do team members show appropriate vulnerability? Do they acknowledge mistakes, apologize and admit shortcomings?

2. Step 2 is to create a grid that has these factors on one axis and the names of your team mates on the other. The grid in our Trust Kit looks like Table 4.6.[58]

Table 4.6 Trust Scorecard (Team Review Grid)

Enter your name and the initials of up to 8 people you work closely with. Assess yourself and your co-workers on each factor. 10 is high/good, 1 is low/bad								
Factor/Name								
Alignment of Interests								
Concern (caring)								
Capability (competency)								
Predictability & Integrity								
Communication & Transparency								
Vulnerability								

3. Step 3 is to assess your trust relationship with each teammate. Use the grid to think through the trust factors with each team member. Rate each factor using a simple 1-to-10 scale. If all the trust factors are 9 or 10, then good. But be very honest with yourself in this assessment: No grade inflation! Only an honest thumbs-up count. If you've given one or more teammates a 6 or lower rating, then use the worksheet shown in Table 4.6 for each of these scores. Write down specifically the nature of the trust issue, such as:
   - Late to meetings consistently
   - Overpromises and underdelivers
   - Takes credit for other people's work

Figure 4.1 Trust Timeline

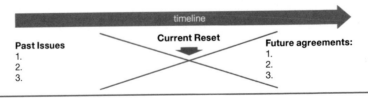

Team members must do a "good enough" job on each of these factors to maintain trust on the team. In our work with intact teams, we describe and explain these factors, then ask team members to confidentially score their colleagues from 1 (poor) to 10 (good) on each factor. Once scored, we ask them to count how many team members they scored 6 or lower on any factor. Finally, we ask them to reveal the number of people they scored 6 or lower by means of a voting slide. An actual result is shown in Table 4.7.

Table 4.7 Sample Voting Slide

How many team members did you score "6" or lower on at least one factor? (10 team members)									
One	Two	Three	Four	Five	Six	Seven	Eight	Nine	None
2	2	3	1	0	0	1	0	1	0

In this case, none of the 10 team members said "Zero." In other words, each team member had at least one trust issue with a teammate. This result is common. FCG has never witnessed a team vote that was perfect; that is, with no trust issues. As you would expect in the messy area of human interaction, things are never perfect. Nevertheless, some firms, while not perfect, have high trust levels, which lead to all the benefits mentioned earlier.

So, what actions do leaders take if they choose to raise trust levels? For example, in the chart in Table 4.7, there is a clear need to work on trust. Several steps are involved:

1. Make the case for why trust is important to performance, as we've attempted to do in this chapter.
2. Determine if "right team members" is the problem. FCG has worked with teams where a change in one member was all that was required to raise trust significantly. Why? Often, it's because trust is predicated on safety.[59] One team member can put safety at risk. If that person is hypercritical or prone to gossip, he or she can make the whole team cautious about open communication and trust.[60] Additionally, we've worked with teams where one person simply wasn't in the right role, and the whole team knew it. Whatever the reason, good leaders need to make tough choices so that the team is happy with "its" members.
3. Check for courage and commitment. Is the team willing to do whatever it takes to strengthen trust? In FCG's experience, many trust issues are not addressed and resolved because team members feel that their colleagues will be offended by attempts to fix trust issues. For this reason, FCG created a voting slide to test this hypothesis. We ask the group: "Would you rather be told about a trust issue or remain in the dark?" When stated this way, team members usually respond, "I'd rather be told!" Table 4.8 is the vote from the same team as in Table 4.7.

Table 4.8 Trust Issue Knowledge Preferences

I would rather KNOW about trust issues with workers than remain the dark	
Agree	100%
Neutral	0%
Disagree	0%

As you can see, all the team members responded, "Yes, I'd rather be told."

4. Cube it. Educate team members about the best way to have "trust-fixing" conversations. Clearly, there are better and worse ways to address trust issues. Saying to a team member, "Hey, can we talk about some of the sleazeball things you do, and why we call you 'Slick Willy'?" will not lead to good outcomes. Rather, it's better to give the conversation some serious prep time, using the model in Figure 4.2.

Figure 4.2 Trust Cube

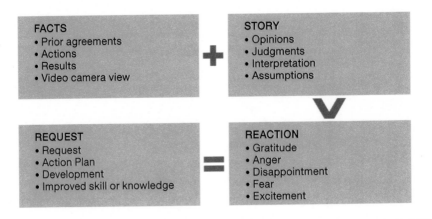

The use of the model is as follows:

Facts: Lead with facts, which may require some research on your part—looking through past agreements, checking emails, and so on. Gain agreement on the facts; that is, make sure they really are facts! Then share them with the other person.

Story: Based on these facts, I formed a story (i.e., an opinion). Share the opinion with the other person. Stop. Let the other person respond. *Is your view accurate? What's the other person's view?*

Reaction: Sometimes it's appropriate to share your reaction: "I was concerned" or "I was confused."

Request: Finally, decide what you want to achieve by having this conversation. Given that we are discussing trust, a logical request would be, "I want to clear up this misunderstanding so that we have a good working relationship, based on strong trust."

In FCG's experience, the underlying problem in most trust issues is a misunderstanding. For example, one trust issue was caused because a team member's emails were inadvertently being rerouted into the junk mail folder. The sender had created a story that the recipient was ignoring the emails. Once the two of them discussed the issue and cleared it up, trust was restored. Often, if team members are simply willing to explore the issue, they will find that their concerns are unfounded. It's rare that a team member is actually trying to pull a fast one and hoping to get away with it!

5. Establish trust partners. Given the importance of trust to success, you want to safeguard against problems. The biggest problem we encounter is blindspots. By definition, you won't see your blindspots (hence, the name!). So, all of us should be committed to feedback from colleagues. In this case we're suggesting a formal trust partner—someone whom you know will provide honest and useful feedback—so that blindspots don't develop. For example, we encountered a situation where one team member was especially sarcastic in meetings. Although his comments often provided humor, many team members felt guarded in the meetings and less than fully trusting around this person. They didn't want to be the target of his biting sarcasm. In this case, one of the FCG coaches pointed out the behavior to the sarcastic person, and the situation improved. However, the same feedback could have been provided by a trust partner on the team. The phenomenon we're describing is a bit like calling for help in a crowd. Research suggests that it is much more effective to point to someone and shout, "Can you help me?" rather than simply to shout, "Someone help!" Likewise, on a team, instead of assuming that someone will point out one's blindspots, it's better to have a designated person who owns that role.

One hope we hold in writing this chapter is to encourage teams to do the work of assembling the right team members to build trust. It requires courage, commitment, and competence (skill). Nearly every good team we've worked with has faced challenges where trust was temporarily damaged. But the best teams put egos aside, roll up their sleeves, and do the work of re-establishing trust.

Let's consider an actual scenario: In a meeting, one of your colleagues seems to take credit for work that you and he did together. You were not present in that meeting. You heard this from someone who was. You feel a little irritation and create the story, "He's trying to take all the credit for our project."

Can you see how easy it would be to let this Trust Fire grow? I mean, it's not a huge deal. Right? But it does raise a concern. These little offences fester and grow. Pretty soon it's a big deal and you are marching south on Gottman's scale. Eventually, you are criticizing or blaming or stonewalling. At that point these trust issues become *much* harder to solve. The house is ablaze. Often, FCG gets called in to put out these fires; unfortunately, despite our best efforts and tools, many are beyond repair.

When you've reflected on and written down the incident that affects trust, then use the cube to get it precise. The cube helps you to get your thinking straight. Let's unpack the previous situation.

- **Set-up**—"I want to put out a possible Trust Fire, because I believe we are both good team members and want to succeed as a team." (Mutual Purpose to establish safety)
- **Facts**—"I'm told that in the meeting, you mentioned the work that you had done on project X. You didn't mention that we worked on that together."
- **Story**—"My story is that our CEO now thinks you did that work on your own."
- **Reaction**—"I was a bit irritated and felt like that created a small Trust Fire. Specifically, that I will not get credit for my contributions when we work together."
- **Request**—"My request is that we share credit fairly for work we've collaborated on. And that you would mention to the CEO that you forgot to state that you and I worked on it together."

After you've cubed your trust concern, express it to your colleague. (Note: you don't need to follow the cube script precisely. Put it in your own words. But lead with facts, *not* your story.) Then you can hear your counterpart's response. Listen carefully to see if there were any misunderstandings. Remember to take full responsibility for your share of the relationship. Perhaps you have been unclear in your agreements. Or perhaps you've developed a reputation that suggests, "You'd better say 'yes' to whatever I ask for... or else!" In other words, you may be unintentionally creating the problem. People may see you as a bully. The goal of the Trust Timeline worksheet (Figure 4.1) is to discuss and let go of the past issues, so that you can do a reset. In the example we've been using, the reset might take the form of a future agreement which sounds like, "I will go to our CEO and let him know that we worked on this project together, in case he misunderstood. And I agree that in the future we should always share credit for joint projects."

From that moment of reset, the key is to monitor and track the new agreements to make sure they are kept. "Trust but verify" is appropriate. Remember to appreciate people who are honoring their agreements. As with any behavior modification, reinforcement is crucial to success. Immediate feedback—using the cube—is important in either direction: success or failure in keeping the new agreement.

You can understand why trust often breaks down in organizations. This maintenance work is awkward, and it *is* work. It takes time and attention—and courage. Most of us are conflict avoidant, and this repair work may feel confrontational. So, to be effective you must continually remind yourself that high-trust environments are crucial to success, and that low-trust environments fuel drama and feel toxic. Then summon your courage and address the issue.

In most cases trust can be repaired if addressed early.[61] Be smart enough to put out the kitchen fires before they become five-alarm blazes. Early detection and treatment is the answer. We hope this Trust Repair Kit will help.

The Trust Repair Kit: FAQ on Trust

1. Is trust a black-and-white issue, or are there shades of gray?

Shades of gray. Sure, there are extremes, but mostly people are in the gray area. In our work, we use a 10-point scale on six factors to measure trust.[62] Remember (from Table 4.6), the factors are:

- Alignment of interests (no major conflicts)
- (Benevolent) Concern (caring)
- Capability (job competence)
- Predictability and integrity (consistency and words/actions lining up)
- Communication and transparency (open communication on a fairly regular basis)
- Vulnerability (willingness to admit mistakes, apologize, acknowledge that you don't know something)

No one ever gets a perfect score: either 60 (i.e., 10 on all six factors) or a 0. In fact, the more relevant measures are the individual scores for the six factors. Typically, a 7 or above on a given factor represents functional levels of trust. So, someone's overall score could be 42 and you could still say, "I trust that person." When an individual score is under 7, then there is usually an issue. For example, on the factor "capability," a score of 6 usually means, "I don't fully trust this person's competence to do a good job."

FCG worked with an investment advisory firm where a partner was unwilling to turn clients over to a subordinate. The reason was capability. The subordinate was excellent on all other measures of trust, but the partner was not convinced that the subordinate had the skill to handle clients on his own. In the partner's view, more time was needed to develop the requisite skills. Alternatively, you may decide that one of the five factors doesn't really matter in assessing your trust of a colleague. For example, in some situations the "frequency" of communication may not be that important. In your mind, you've established the other person as very trustworthy on the first four factors, and it doesn't matter that you rarely communicate with her. Shades of gray is one of the most important reasons we use the six factors and a 10-point scale. Determining why you may or may not fully trust someone is a worthwhile pursuit to begin solving the trust dilemma.

2. What about when the trust issue is with your boss?

Good question—and sometimes sticky. This question highlights the importance of a Google study on its best teams.[63] Google found that the key commonality of great teams was "psychological safety." This phrase means that the team members felt safe to be themselves, to show up as real and candid, to take risks. Bosses who create this trusting and safe environment have much more engaged and productive team members. Hence, for years FCG has been working with investment leaders to create trust and safety on teams. The Google study was a wonderful affirmation of our framework.

So, back to the question. What kind of environment has your boss created? There are three basic levels:

- **Functional trust**. If the trust level is functional, that means you score your boss pretty highly on the Trust Scorecard (see Table 4.6). There is enough safety to raise the trust issue directly. Use the tools provided earlier in this chapter to repair trust.
- **Dysfunctional trust**. In this scenario, which is common, the boss would have one or more scores of 6 or below on the trust indicator. For example, the boss may be very competent and genuinely caring but may have a blindspot around agreements. Perhaps he overpromises and underdelivers (leading to a lower score on predictability/integrity), and does so on a regular basis. It's a pattern: Hence, the dysfunction. So, again, you could use the tools described in this chapter to repair trust and work through the issue with the boss. Have your facts well documented and approach the conversation in a constructive way.

Alternatively, you may assess the situation as a bit more entrenched. The boss is basically a decent person but he has strong defenses against acknowledging any weaknesses. He is world class at denial! "I can understand why the behavior you describe would be troublesome, but I don't do it!" In this case, you might want to get a skillful third party involved (this lessens the career risk for you!). Many firms have resources, such as Human Resource departments, that have the ability and the authority to step in and help. You can brainstorm your situation with the third parties and see if they have a suggestion for how to raise the trust issue effectively. Often, they know the boss and his personality and can approach the person in a nonthreatening way. One technique that we've seen work is to generalize the trust issue to the team level, and then tackle it as a team. Once the dialogue is started with the team, it may be easier for each person to take responsibility for her or his contribution to building/eroding trust. If several team members express the same issue—overpromising and underdelivering—then possibly you will break through the defenses and get the boss to see the problem...his problem! A key to success in bringing up the issue will be using the cube methodology we presented in the Trust Repair kit in the first section of this chapter. Leading the discussion with facts will begin to remove the emotion from the discussion and give you the opportunity to present factual situations that may be blindspots for your boss.

- **No safety/No trust**. Unfortunately, this situation exists all too frequently. Bosses who are very insecure are prone to retaliation. Instead of listening to the employee's concern and then rationally dealing with it, they lash out in retaliation. Usually, a well-intentioned effort by the employee to address trust issues turns out badly. Unless there is strong support—say, from senior management—we don't advocate a heroic approach to "fixing" the boss. If this is the case, you may be facing a career decision. Ultimately, people join organizations and leave bosses. If it becomes clear that your boss does not want to build a trusting relationship, then you may decide that you need to work for someone else in the same firm, or (if that is not possible) leave the firm. If you stay, you are consciously deciding to take part in a "villain/victim" drama, in which the boss plays the schoolyard bully, and you play the hapless victim. Sometimes life circumstances call for you to do this ("I need this job right now"). Okay, but commit to finding some better arrangement as soon as you can. Or, acknowledge the nature of the boss—villain personality—and resolve *not* to sink into drama. In other words, don't play victim. Some people's personality type allows them to do this without taking on too much stress (the Buddha, the Dalai Lama, Mother Teresa, to name a few …)

For the bosses reading this piece, remember that psychological safety is a key characteristic of top teams. You want to create a team environment where team members feel safe raising issues and providing feedback. If you don't create this environment, you'll have lower engagement, reduced productivity, and flight risk. To create safety, you as the boss must have sufficient confidence and security to hear feedback without getting defensive. Remember, the three big reasons we get defensive are because one of the following is threatened: security, approval, or control. Learn to manage these needs, so you can hear feedback. (Employees: you may want to copy this chapter and leave it on the boss's desk … anonymously!)

3. Do I have to respect someone to trust them?

Interesting. Oxford defines respect as "a feeling of deep admiration for someone or something elicited by their abilities, qualities, or achievements."[64] Using this definition, no. You don't need to deeply admire someone to trust them. As long as they pass the six factors, then you probably will trust them. There is a slight nuance to this consideration: FCG believes that strong cultures are often built on the value of *respect*. However, this does not mean a deep admiration; instead, it means that you will treat *all* people with dignity and respect, regardless of your judgments about them. In this definition of *respect*, you might treat them with respect but *not* trust them.

4. If someone violates trust, can it really be reestablished?

Yes. That's the point of our earlier discussion on building and maintaining trust. If you catch trust issues early, then you can address them before they become irreversible. FCG has found that early diagnosis and treatment works. Unfortunately, too many people let the trust issues compound and then revel in the judgment that "I was right. He IS untrustworthy!" (Again, Ego loves to be right.) Of course, the problem with this approach is confirmation bias. Once we have a hypothesis that someone is untrustworthy, we look for evidence to make our case, plus we talk to people who will support it. Trust repair goes the other direction: confront the person directly, using the cube, and clean up the misunderstanding. In FCG's experience, only a handful of people are pathologically untrustworthy. The rest of us are simply human and make mistakes. So, reestablishing trust should be the norm, not the exception.

5. Do I have to trust someone to work with him?

I believe the intent of the question is: Do I have to trust someone to work *effectively* with him? FCG's experience indicates yes. A lot of mental energy is wasted when you work with untrustworthy people. You worry about deadlines, work product, backstabbing, gossip, and a host of other petty concerns. I can say I am blessed to work with my team members at FCG because I waste virtually *no* time with these concerns. Warren Buffett has made similar statements. He simply won't work with people he does not trust. His deals are done on a handshake.

Here is the summary of key ideas concerning trust:

1. Understand that trust is crucial to strong and sustainable performance.
2. Monitor trust with co-workers. (Use the scorecard provided in this chapter, Table 4.6.)

3. Recognize that a predictable decline occurs if trust issues are left untreated.
4. Deal with trust issues when they are small and "easy." Don't wait until they are serious (like medicine: early diagnosis and treatment).
5. Use the cube to describe prior issues in a "clean" (nonblaming) way.
6. Get current: let go of past issues and make agreements about future behavior.
7. Monitor new agreements and build "new" trust over time.

Trust is core to the investment industry and to healthy functioning of teams. Treat trust issues like kitchen fires: jump on them and fix them immediately. Work to build a safe and trusting environment.

Trust is one of three key elements of high-performing teams. Let's cover teamwork next and discuss the other two factors.

---

55 For more on these firms, read our white paper, "Linking Culture to Success," http://www.focuscgroup.com/wp-content/uploads/2015/11/Linking_Strong_Culture_to_Success.pdf
56 For a short, excellent video, watch John Gottman, "How to Build Trust," https://www.youtube.com/watch?v=rgWnadSi91s
57 Adapted from Robert F. Hurley, "The Decision to Trust," *Harvard Business Review* (September 2006).
58 The kit is available from Liz at lseveryns@focuscgroup.com.
59 For more on this, see Charles Duhigg, "What Google Learned from Its Quest to Build the Perfect Team," *New York Times Magazine* (February 25, 2016), exploring Google's excellent research on common factors of high-performing teams at Google; https://www.nytimes.com/2016/02/28/magazine/what-google-learned-from-its-quest-to-build-the-perfect-team.html?smid=pl-share
60 See Appendix A for the factors relating to trust.
61 If the trust issue has reached the "stonewalling" or "contempt" level, then a third party may be needed for an intervention. FCG has successfully facilitated sessions like these. So, don't give up hope. But if things have gotten really bad, bring in a neutral and skilled third party to repair the trust issue.
62 For the full version, see the Trust Scorecard in Table 4.6.
63 Duhigg, "What Google Learned from Its Quest to Build the Perfect Team," https://www.nytimes.com/2016/02/28/magazine/what-google-learned-from-its-quest-to-build-the-perfect-team.html?smid=pl-share
64 Oxford Dictionaries, https://en.oxforddictionaries.com/definition/respect

CHAPTER 5

Teams: Where the Work Gets Done

T eams are the basic unit of a firm. Overall firm performance is the aggregation of the individual teams. Staff members relate much more to their team than to the overall firm. Hence, assembling and leading teams is crucial to employee engagement, retention, and performance.

FCG has worked with teams around the world and collected data to assess the factors that lead to success. FCG administers Team Scorecards to intact teams to see how they are performing on 24 well-researched factors that contribute to success.[65] These factors fit into our overall model for team success:

Good process (hard skills) + good relationship (soft skills) = Quality results[66]

Our Team Scorecard measures these factors on two dimensions:

1. **Skill:** Is the team GOOD at a particular factor?
2. **Importance:** Does the team VALUE a particular factor?

The scorecard summarizes the results by highlighting the factors that are deemed very important, but were scored low on the skill rating. For example, a team result might show that team members really value candor (high importance), but also indicate that they are not very good at it (low skill). The clear recommendation in this case is: Take action to create more candor on the team.

Detailed datasets are included in Appendix A, as our goal is to keep this chapter clear and practical (you're welcome!).

Let's start with the three factors that are deemed most important to quality results. From the 220 team members (across 28 teams) who completed the Team Scorecard (anonymously), these factors were considered mission critical:

1. **Clear Purpose and Direction:** I know what our team is trying to achieve and why.
2. **Right Team Members:** We have the right individuals to accomplish our goals.
3. **Trust:** I trust the people on our team.

Leaning on the "wisdom of crowds" principle, we assume that there is wisdom in this collective vote. It makes intuitive sense. Team members are saying, "In order to produce quality results, we must get these factors right." Hence, the equation for success becomes:

Clear purpose and direction + Right team members + Trust = Quality results[67]

In previous chapters, we covered purpose and trust, so here we will focus on the factor: right team members. This factor includes *wrong* team members as well. We have coined the term *Red X* for these people. Often, they are very talented and produce results, but they create friction in a team. Leaders must then decide if the friction outweighs the good results. Further, leaders must assess the cultural implications of a Red X. If the behavior of the Red X is tolerated or overlooked, the firm is essentially sending the message that it is okay to break the rules as long you produce: the end justifies the means. We'll cover Red Xs—an important issue for teams—in Chapter 6.

Right Team Members

Assembling the right team members is crucial to success because it drives so many other factors, including our third factor, trust.[68] In FCG's experience, we've found that the ideal team player has the following characteristics:[69]

1. **Curious** and humble, often with an analytical bent. These qualities in a team member contribute to good listening, patience, diligence, and safety. This quality allows such team members to choose inquiry over defensiveness. They seek learning/understanding over being right. The downside of this personality trait is that they can become doormats, if they don't have the other two characteristics.
2. **Driven.** Good team players have a drive to succeed. They are appropriately ambitious, with a push for continuous improvement and excellence. This quality provides a natural desire for accountability, and a no-nonsense drive for direct communication and clarity. The driver who lacks the other two characteristics can become a bulldozer, seeking control and running over people.
3. **Relational.** A final quality of an ideal team player is emotional intelligence. These members have enough self-awareness to understand themselves and enough other-awareness to read their teammates. In this sense, they are people-smart. However, if they are solely motivated by relational qualities, they may simply be schmoozers: smooth but ineffective.

The catch in finding an ideal team member is that she or he must have all three characteristics. If that's not the case, then you will frequently end up with the red-lettered problems in the Venn diagram in Figure 5.1.

Figure 5.1 Ideal Team Player

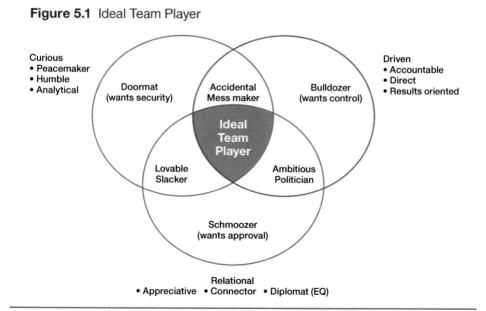

If a team member has only one characteristic, he or she may be a Doormat, Bulldozer, or Schmoozer. But even two characteristics is not enough.

If team members are *curious* and *driven*, but not *relational*, they can end up causing unintended messes. For example, they are curious about a new process and driven to design and execute it, but they are wholly unaware of the effect it will have on other parts of the organization. With all good intentions, they nevertheless create a mess.

Similarly, if team members are *curious* and *relational*, they might be delightful to work with—friendly, smart, and safe—but ineffective in getting things done. They are complacent. They lack the drive, or the courage, —to push forward and make things happen.

Finally, the combination of *relational* and *driven* can be the most dangerous of all, because this combination allows for ambition and finesse. These people can be working a private agenda without anyone knowing it. They can be sneaky in this way (think: Machiavelli), and they lack the humility and curiosity to put the team and firm first. Often these characters are the hardest to spot.

At first glance, it may seem overly ambitious to find individuals who have all three of these qualities: curious, driven, and relational. But FCG has worked with teams that are comprised of such individuals, and to our delight, we believe that FCG's team members all have these qualities. So, in looking to assemble a team, leaders can use these guidelines for selection. Find team members who have a sufficient level of skill in each area. The good news is that people can improve in any of these areas. They are *learnable skills*. A key to learning the three qualities of ideal team players is emotional intelligence (EQ).

Emotional intelligence, defined and described in the works of Dan Goleman, is the skillset that allows us to know ourselves and others better. We can accurately assess which of the ideal skillsets we have, and which require work. If we are emotionally intelligent (have a high emotional intelligence quotient or EQ), then we know our own thoughts and feelings (are self-aware) and we can identify others' thoughts and feelings. If we add to those skills our ability to manage ourselves—take a breath, say, before we shout at a co-worker—and skillfully interact with others, we have high EQ. In short, EQ is the ability to handle interpersonal matters well. Investment firms are chock-full of employees who have towering IQs and relatively tiny EQs. (Evidence suggests that "intelligence tests are not necessarily good predictors of success generally."[70]) One way to think of the research on IQ versus EQ is: IQ gets you in the door, but EQ makes you successful. Years ago, Bell Labs researched this topic and found that their star performers had EQ, though they didn't have this term back then. The benefits? Stars got phone calls returned and favors granted. They were influencers who had greased the wheels of effectiveness. High IQ *and* high EQ. Everyone who gets past the gatekeepers at an investment firm—gets hired—is smart. The ones who contribute the most are both smart and people-savvy. They make great leaders, teammates, and client-facing professionals. EQ is so important that we've devoted the last chapter (Chapter 8) to this topic.

Another aspect of strong teams is sufficient cognitive diversity. *Cognitive diversity* refers to the way people see the world, think, and make decisions. It differs from identity diversity, which involves race, ethnicity, gender, and the like. The definitive book on why cognitive diversity matters is by Scott Page: *The Difference: How the Power of Diversity Creates Better Groups, Firms, Schools, and Societies.*[71] In this exhaustive study, Page defines and proves two points:[72]

1. **Diversity trumps homogeneity**: collections of people with diverse perspectives and heuristics outperform collections of people who rely on homogeneous perspectives and heuristics.
2. **Diversity trumps ability**: random collections of intelligent problem solvers can outperform the best individual problem solvers (i.e., diverse teams win).

With a multitude of empirical data, Page shows that[73]

- Diverse perspectives and tools enable collections of people to find more and better solutions and contribute to overall productivity.
- Diverse predictive models enable crowds of people to predict values accurately.

In our experience, the investment industry consistently uses a flawed approach, which Page addresses:

> [W]hen confronted with a difficult task, be it solving a problem, predicting the future, or making a choice, we benefit by including diverse people. In such situations, we might think about gathering together the best and brightest minds, but that's a flawed approach. We also need to pay attention to the diversity of those minds, all the more so if the old saying that "great minds think alike" holds true.[74]

Indeed, in our experience we see repeatedly that the cognitive diversity on investment teams is limited. Especially on the investment side of the house, we see teams that are overwhelmingly comprised of the type we mentioned earlier: Driver. Undoubtedly, these individuals have a tremendous amount of talent and drive, but a team comprised of mainly this type will lose to a diverse team of equally smart and well-trained professionals.

Page is thorough in his research and cites many studies, concluding:

> *Studies of creativity and innovation conclude that cognitive variation is a key explanatory variable. Studies also show that management teams with greater training and experiential diversity typically introduce more innovations. Based on this evidence, organizational scholars generally agree that cognitive diversity improves rates of innovation.*[75]

Page sums up his chapter on the benefits of cognitive diversity by saying, "The benefits of diversity do exist. They're real, and over time, if we can leverage them, we'll be far better off. We'll find better solutions to our problems. We'll make better predictions."[76]

However, Page is not so naïve as to think that talent does not matter. He writes: "We should not forget that ability still matters. Ability matters as much as diversity. If you want a super duper basketball team, draft Michael Jordan even if you have to sacrifice some diversity."[77]

Therefore, Page does not advocate sacrificing ability for diversity, but rather balancing the two. Here's the catch (there is always a catch, right?): more cognitive diversity often leads to more conflict. Page acknowledges that "diversity produces better outcomes but more conflict."[78] And that's why the EQ is necessary for high-performing teams: they need increased emotional intelligence (EQ) to manage the conflict.

But how do you measure cognitive diversity?

The Enneagram is a powerful tool in helping both staff members and leaders increase their EQ. It provides them with a blueprint of how they are hard-wired. Am I more inclined to action or reflection? Am I optimistic or pessimistic? Am I more aggressive or more passive? Do I pay attention to precision and details, or do I prefer creative, big-picture thinking? Am I more a pack animal or a lone wolf? Am I better with people or ideas? These insights help us know our own attitudes and behaviors better. But they also broaden our worldview such that we begin to understand why others think and behave differently. These insights can be especially helpful in managing our relationships on a cognitively diverse team. We can begin to understand and even appreciate the power of differences. We can begin to leverage them.

Although the Enneagram is wonderfully rich and deep, it does not require an advanced degree to prove useful. Most people can apply its lessons immediately. And that's what we'll explore next.

FCG uses the Enneagram personality assessment to measure this aspect of a team. Of the 9 basic personality types, we hope to see at least 5 on a team of 10 people. The team shown in Figure 5.2, an actual leadership team, has a good blend of cognitive diversity.[79]

Figure 5.2 Cognitive Diversity

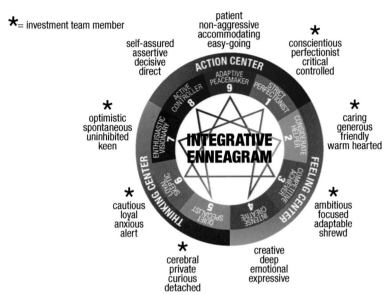

The two big levers we are talking about—diversity and EQ—lead to several benefits in an investment firm. Cognitive diversity allows more intelligent hiring; that is, acquiring talent that adds to the firm's diversity—and the diversity itself leads to better decision making. Higher EQ allows for a variety of benefits: higher trust and respect levels, better communication (including more skillful feedback), and more savvy leaders, and therefore better teamwork, more skillful coaching and mentoring, and a reduction in conflict (or at least more skill in addressing it). Not to mention better client interactions.

The toughest problem for leaders is dealing with a team member who doesn't seem to fit. Sometimes this challenge involves good corporate citizens (culture fits) who have legitimate differences. For example, FCG worked with a fundamental research team in which one of the team members handled the quantitative filters. Over time, this individual became increasingly convinced that the fundamental efforts were adding little value. It was the upfront quantitative screens that chose the winning stocks. The team leader described it as having a "Buddhist attending Christian services." Neither was right nor wrong, just a wholly different view. In this case, the leader moved the quantitative member off the team.

Assembling the right team members requires leaders to pay close attention to the team dynamics, especially with members who don't fit. FCG has developed a number of assessments to help leaders make this call: 360 reviews, individual interviews, and the Team Scorecard are useful. In borderline cases, FCG favors the approach of giving the "non-fit" person the opportunity to change, through direct feedback and possibly coaching. If that doesn't work, though, our experience has clearly shown that leaders must move that person off the team.

Another aspect of "right" teams is that they align people's strengths with their roles. It's one thing to assemble a team of talented people who trust, respect, and appreciate one another; it's another thing to have them strongly engaged and effective. We worked with one analyst team in which a major upgrade was achieved by allowing the industrials analyst and the consumer analyst to change roles. They had each covered the other sector at a prior firm and really had passion for the switch. Results improved after the change.

One hope we hold in writing this chapter is to encourage teams to do the work of clearly defining their mission, assembling the right team members, and building trust. It requires courage, commitment, and competence (skill). Given the effort involved, a fair question is "Does it work?" Do teams get better results when they have strong purpose, right team members, and high trust?

Our data suggest that yes, this happens. When we look at the teams that have high-quality results scores and then look at their "right team" and "trust" scores, we find the data in Table 5.1.

Table 5.1 Team Performance Elements

Team	Quality Results	Rank	Right Team Members	Rank	Trust People on Team	Rank
Firm 1	6.25	1	6.00	5	6.50	3
Firm 2	6.25	1	5.75	8	6.50	3
Firm 3	6.00	3	6.00	5	6.20	7
Firm 4	5.93	4	6.07	4	6.33	5
Firm 5	5.75	5	6.50	1	6.75	1
Firm 24	4.17	24	4.25	25	4.00	26
Firm 25	4.00	25	4.14	27	4.57	22
Firm 26	3.80	26	5.60	11	4.00	26
Firm 27	3.33	27	4.33	23	4.17	25
Firm 28	3.25	28	4.58	20	5.45	18

Top 5 firms shown in blue, bottom 5 firms shown in orange

Indeed, the top results belong to the teams that have high scores across both right members and trust, whereas the opposite is true of the lowest scores for results. A chi-square test looking at quality results against right team members and trust confirmed these findings, with the analysis showing that there is a measurable difference between Top-5 and non-Top-5 results firms across these factors.[80]

So, yes, the hard work of "doing" the Big Three (clear purpose and direction, right team members, and trust) *does* work. It produces quality results.

Before moving on to the Red X—those team members who can disrupt a team's performance—let's recap our results so far. FCG's extensive work with teams has revealed three key factors of success. The teams that produce quality results get these three pieces right:

1. A clear purpose and direction
2. The right team members
3. A high level of trust

When these three factors are in place, they drive the following outcomes for the team:

• Different ideas and opinions are respected
• Candor and openness prevail
• Open and productive debates occur
• Conflict is addressed and resolved

Additionally, these favorable factors are highly correlated with the three other success factors:

• Growth and development
• Clear decision authority
• Team spirit

To put it in simple language, a team leader must explain to her or his team: "Here's where we're going and why" (clear direction and purpose). Using a mountain-climbing analogy, "We're going to scale this mountain. On the summit, we will find the following valuable items: X, Y, and Z. These items are valuable because … . There are a variety of paths we could take, and we've chosen the Northern route for the following reasons: A, B, C." Good leaders understand the importance of clarifying the mission (the "why"), the vision (the "where"), and the strategy (the "how"). Make sure all team members understand and buy into all of these.

To achieve quality results (i.e., scale the mountain), leaders must assemble the **right team members**: the right skills, the right culture fit, good chemistry. Cognitive diversity helps considerably. Challenging team members—Red Xs—require leaders to make a "fix it or fold it" decision. Ignoring the problem is a recipe for disappointment (more on this in Chapter 6).

Finally, trust must be built and maintained. Trust issues will creep in over time, so leaders must constantly "weed the garden." Watch for trust issues and encourage team members to address them early, while they are small. Blindspots are the biggest derailer. We all need reliable feedback to avoid damaging trust. Formal trust partners can serve a valuable function.

Much of what we've said is common sense. The Big Three factors are not mysterious new findings. However, we know, based on mathematical rigor and our client experience, that these factors really matter to quality results. The successful firms get them right—and getting them right is the tough part. It requires tough decisions and hard work. We've offered suggestions for how to do just that. We applaud the teams that have the courage, commitment, and skill to do it.

---

[65] See Appendix 5A for a list of all 24 factors.

[66] Quality results are defined by each team separately because the nature of results relates to a firm's function. For example, for an investment team, the term refers to superior investment results. For a client-facing team, it relates to client retention and satisfaction.

[67] See Appendix 5B, Figure 5B.1.

[68] See chapter 4.

[69] Thanks to Patrick Lencioni for introducing us to these ideas, which we've restated in FCG terms.

[70] Scott Page, *The Difference: How the Power of Diversity Creates Better Groups, Firms, Schools, and Societies* (Princeton University Press, 2007), p. 127.

[71] Page, *The Difference*.

[72] *Ibid.*, p. 10.

[73] *Ibid.*, p. 13.

[74] *Ibid.*, p. 17.

[75] *Ibid.*, p. 323.

[76] *Ibid.*, p. 335.

[77] *Ibid.*, p. 363.

[78] *Ibid.*, p. 299.

[79] For more on cognitive diversity, see Michael Mauboussin and Dan Callahan, "Building and Effective Team" (January 8, 2014), https://research-doc.credit-suisse.com/docView?language=ENG&format=PDF&source_id=csplusresearchcp&document_id=1027591531&serialid=%2BeSRZFAZXAxDxS9Isv8h6jQCVcQyYenZFVI5smWZpRE%3D

[80] See Appendix 5B, Figures 5B.4 and 5B.5.

Appendix 5A

Factors Contributing to Success

- We have a clear purpose and direction. I know what our team is trying to achieve.
- I know my role on the team and what is expected of me.
- I have the resources I need to do my work well.
- We have the right team members to accomplish our goals.
- I feel valued and appreciated for my work.
- I trust the people on our team.
- I experience a high level of candor and openness on our team.
- I feel fairly paid for my contributions.
- I have clear performance goals that measure my success on this team.
- I receive useful feedback from my leader.
- We have open and productive debates.
- My work allows me to use my talents and abilities.
- My leader encourages my growth and development.
- I feel that my work is important to reaching our firm's goals.
- The team consistently produces quality results; we deliver on our promises.
- The strategies for achieving our goals are clear and agreed upon.
- We have common values and norms that promote good teamwork.
- The team celebrates successes and milestones.
- Conflict is addressed and resolved in a constructive way; we know how to "deal with it" and move on.
- Different ideas, opinions, feelings, and perspectives from all team members are respected.
- Decision authority is clearly assigned; we know who makes which decisions.
- I have a strong sense of pride in our team's accomplishments.
- The team has developed good processes to make us both effective and efficient.
- We have a strong sense of team spirit; we feel a sense of connection.

Appendix 5B

Table 5B.1 Factors Driving Quality Results

The team consistently produces quality results, we deliver on our promises.	
We have the right team members	0.49
I trust the people on our team	0.48
Purpose and direction	0.36

Table 5B.2 Right Team Members: Team Average

We have the right team members.	
We have the right team members	1.00
I trust the people on our team	0.65
Common values	0.61
Candor and openness	0.59
Team spirit	0.51
Quality results	0.49
Conflict is addressed	0.46

Table 5B.3 Skill: Team Average

I trust the people on our team.	
I trust the people on our team	1.00
Candor and openness	0.87
Common values	0.83
Conflict is addressed	0.83
Team spirit	0.82
Open and productive debates	0.74
Ideas are respected	0.68
We have the right team members	0.65
Growth and development	0.56
Decision and authority	0.53
Quality results	0.48

CHAPTER 6

Difficult People: The Red X

A bout 80% of investment firms acknowledge having Red Xs. Hopefully, the remaining 20% will come out of denial soon. FCG coined the term *Red X*: it means a talented star who is difficult to manage and prickly to work with. Many of our assignments involve helping senior leaders deal with Red Xs. Many of the senior leaders *are* Red Xs (and don't know it). This is a tricky aspect of the Red X problem: most people don't self-identify as a Red X. FCG routinely shows this slide to audiences. It's an investment firm's executive committee (EC), which readily acknowledged that there were multiple Red Xs on the EC but when asked, "Are YOU the Red X?" responded as shown in Table 6.1.

Table 6.1 Red X Self Assessment

Do you consider yourself a Red X (London Team)	
Yes	0%
No	100%

There you have it: the problem in a nutshell. So, let's get more precise about defining and dealing with Red Xs. Most firms acknowledge having them, which is understandable because in a talent business, you need top talent. But what exactly are Red Xs?

Enter the book on *Leading Clever People*[81] by Goffee and Jones (hereafter "Gojo") of the London Business School. Many of the best books I read are recommended by clients, and this one was suggested by Emilio Gonzalez, CEO of BT Investment Management. Over dinner in Sydney, Emilio explained how this book had given him insights about how to manage the clever people (Red Xs) in his organization. I read it and agree. So, I will present Gojo's research on clever people (from all industries) and then comment on how it fits with our experience in the investment world. Note: Not all clever people are Red Xs. Some Red Xs are benign: odd and difficult to manage but not toxic. And then again, some superstars are delightful and great collaborators. But they are the exception, not the rule.

Gojo define "clever people" as follows:

> Clever people are highly talented individuals with the potential to create disproportionate amounts of value from the resources that the organization makes available to them.

Gojo add that we are not talking about solo artists, but rather talented people who need an organization to achieve full potential. This point is important. Many Red Xs are rather oblivious to this point: they believe that they could do it alone, and generally regard co-workers as kind of a nuisance. One CEO put it this way: "Clever people might not feel that they need the firm, and they might feel that they've got enough brains to do all sorts of other things, but the fact is, they stay. They feel they've got room to do what it is they need to do and that they might be vulnerable if they weren't in the firm. There is a protection element in the firm, even though they might hold it in contempt."[82] This statement rings true in FCG's experience. One star PM who is currently wrestling with his CEO for more compensation mirrors this situation exactly. He continually brings in evidence from other firms that he is underpaid relative to the other firms' stars, to which his CEO responds, "We are paying you as much as we can without breaking our financial model. If you want the higher pay, you'll have to go to one of those firms." The PM stays put but continues to complain.

Interestingly, Gojo believe—and we agree—that the clever people will stay "if you can offer them a great place in which to express their cleverness and other clever people to work with." Then they make a very important conclusion for the compensation issue:

> Even in companies that have high-compensation strategies for clever people, good promotion prospects, and exciting projects to work on, the difference between a high retention rate of the most talented and an average retention rate is in how they are led.[83]

Uh-oh. Now the onus is back on you, the leader. So, let's explore the characteristics of Red Xs and how best to lead them.

First, what are the common characteristics of a clever person? Gojo list nine, and here I review them as they relate to the investment world.

1. **Cleverness is central to their identity.** They *are* their work. Their passion for their work defines them, and they identify with their craft, *not* the firm. They are driven and often perfectionistic about their work. They want to get it just right. They don't like relying on others, so they tend to be poor team players. They want to believe that their own cleverness can get the job done. Sometimes their independence creates a hostility toward the firm.

   FCG comment: *True and false. We see this very often with star analysts or PMs. They love their work, want to win, and don't suffer fools lightly. Their chief loyalty is to the investment craft. They are often prepared to leave and join another firm or start their own shop. However, we have encountered some star investors who are quite loyal and do identify with their firm. Often the founder of the firm is the star PM and is completely loyal to the firm she or he started.*

2. **Their skills are not easily replicated.** The knowledge of clever people is tacit. It is embedded in them. A great deal of their cleverness resides not in *what* they know but *who* they know and *how* they know it.

   FCG comment: *Indeed—and this is one of the dirty little secrets in the investment world. Many investment processes cannot be replicated because they do rely on one clever person. Bigger organizations—like a PIMCO with Bill Gross gone—may* *have enough quality bench strength to fill in. But many firms that we work with have investment teams of five people: one seriously clever person, with four analysts who help with research. In our view, it is often the case that none of the four researchers could replace the star PM.*

3. **They know their worth.** This point follows from point #2. If the clever person is truly good, then chances are he knows that his skills are unique. This is a challenge for leaders: Confident in their own worth and ability, clever people exert pressure on their leaders. Their skepticism about the value of leadership puts pressure on leaders to demonstrate their worth.

   FCG comment: *True—which is why leading clever people in investment firms is so challenging. And why compensation negotiations can be so difficult. (It doesn't matter what experts say you are worth, clever people will debate it, and debate it skillfully. FCG's work in compensation appreciates this aspect of clever people and involves skillful mediation about what fair compensation means. You must get the clever person to buy in.)*

4. **They ask difficult questions.** They are passionate and willing to debate. In fact, many CEOs consider this a prerequisite for "clever" status": You must be willing to defend your ideas. Challenging assumptions and cherished beliefs is what makes clever people so valuable.

   FCG comment: *Especially in the investment world. This point is amplified by the nature of markets: in order to win, you must see things differently from the rest of the world. You must be willing to challenge conventional views. The leader's role is to live with the discomfort that accompanies this dissident thinking, and even to appreciate it. Despite their challenging personalities, clever people still want to be valued for their contributions. Their egos still need stroking. Even though they deny it!*

5. **They are organizationally savvy.** Clever people are expert gamers. They typically don't like politics, but when their hands are forced, they can engage and play with the best of them.

   FCG comment: *I had to think about this one. My initial thought was, "No, most clever investment people are rather naïve about office politics." But as I mentally inventoried the many clever people we've worked with, I realized that they are good politicians when they need to be. Especially in the investment world, because they understand tradeoffs very well, and they understand game theory, and they are smart.*

6. **They don't like hierarchy and don't want to be led.** If there is one thing that defines clever people, it is that they don't want to be led, and they are absolutely certain they don't want to be managed! They have an undisguised disdain for organizational hierarchy as captured in the org chart. They don't give a hoot about titles. You've got to influence them through your skill and knowledge. At the end of the day, they are a "show me" group of elitists. Smart leaders know that you cannot lead these clever people; the best you can do is guide them—gently—in the desired direction. They are likely to be motivated by factors other than money and power.

   FCG comment: *Well, not entirely. Money is a measuring stick for them, and the star PMs seem acutely aware of what "winning" and "losing" compensation packages look like. Performing well and then getting a big bonus is the equivalent of scoring a touchdown and then spiking the ball in the end zone. If you deprive PMs of their victory dance and spike, they don't like it. After all, it is a money industry, so the generic rules for clever people—about money—are a little different in the investment arena. Money does matter as a metric of success. As to being led, the advice absolutely applies: don't make the mistake of thinking that investment professionals will gladly salute and carry out orders. They would more likely give you the one-finger salute than carry out your orders. This is where the skill is required from investment leaders; they must know how to lead "softly" through influence, not orders.*

7. **They expect instant access.** Clever people are very absorbed in their own thinking, so when they get a great idea they want it considered immediately. Clever people have very low boredom thresholds. *Very low.* They tend to hate needless meetings. They are very conscious of the value of their time.

   FCG comment: *Absolutely true. Fortunately for PMs, they often get to act immediately on their ideas, which is very gratifying to them. Unfortunately for analysts, they often do not get to act immediately on their ideas, and thus end up frustrated. CIOs and PMs need to keep in this mind as they manage a research team. The analysts consider themselves clever, and want to play by the same rules that other clever people enjoy. Smart CIO/PMs will give them as much freedom and access as they possibly can.*

8. **They want to be connected to other clever people.** Clever people need other clever people to achieve their full potential. Even the most self-absorbed PMs will grudgingly acknowledge that they need good ideas and good research to win. Clever people need others; they need organizations to plug into. Clever people enjoy networking with like-minded or like-qualified individuals. For clever people, networking is not a social nicety but a source of perpetual improvement and bright ideas.

FCG comment: *Yes and no. Certainly the PMs and analysts that we know have their sources for good ideas (some internal, some external). However, the biggest "ask" that we get from large, global firms is: How do we get our bright people talking to one another, so as to get some synergies? One firm FCG has worked with leads the pack in this respect. How? They have done it through technology. One of their senior investment people also has expertise in IT and has helped them develop a very user-friendly intranet that allows them to share investment research in a powerful way. This firm was able to cite many examples of investment triumphs via this rich exchange of ideas. For most firms, though, it is hit or miss. Mostly miss.*

9. **They won't thank you.** "There's a part of me, a slightly dark part of me, that thinks these clever people wouldn't recognize management or leadership if you hit them in the face with it,"[84] one slightly forlorn leader confided. (Sound familiar?) This may be true, but it gets to the heart of the challenge. Clever people might respond that leaders wouldn't easily recognize great science, a world-changing computer program, or even an innovative new coffee machine if it were thrust before them. As Gojo say, "you know you're a success when you hear the clever people say you're not getting in the way too much."[85]

FCG comment: *We smiled when we read this part. For years we've been saying that the investment industry suffers from ADD: Appreciation Deficit Disorder. Despite the emerging neuroscientific research concerning the brain and gratitude—being appreciated—few investment leaders or practitioners have changed their behavior much. When we ask CIOs why they are so stingy with their praise, we get responses like: "Well, we pay them, don't we!?" or "If we praise them, they'll ask for more money." And our favorite one: "If we praise them, they'll stop working so hard." Sorry, but those beliefs are just wrong. Our experience—and the neuroscience—point in the opposite direction: appreciate and value your staff and they will work harder, demand less money, and be far more loyal.*

So, there have it: the defining characteristics of clever people. Most of these apply to Red Xs. So, what do you do as leaders to manage these unmanageable stars?

If you can't manage or lead them, what can you do? In presentations to investment audiences, we've presented this voting slide to find out what investment leaders actually do real-time. Here are the results from the invstment industry (Table 6.2).

Table 6.2 How do you typically manage Red Xs (choose 2)

	Investment Industry
Fix 'em	16
Fall in love with 'em	13
Fret about 'em	15
Firewall 'em	15
Fire 'em	25
Forget about 'em	26

Notice that all the choices are represented in the voting results. There are many ways to deal with Red Xs. Choices "Fret about 'em" and "Forget about 'em" are basically the good old "stick your head in the sand and hope the problem goes away" strategy (*denial* is not just a river in Egypt). Usually leaders include a little "hinting and hoping" in those strategies. Which is comical because we all know that little, gentle nudges will have the same effect on these people as on your favorite dictator (insert name here): *Nada*.

Then there is the "Fix 'em" option, which is where FCG comes in. We routinely get hired to come in and assess the situation and coach the Red Xs. (In one case, after the firm had fired the Red X twice and hired him back a third time, FCG got the call. Raise your hand if you think that in this instance—three's a charm—the Red X had changed his stripes. Of course not!) In this case, we quickly moved from "Fix 'em" to "Firewall 'em". The firm removed all his direct reports, located the Red X 35 miles from the headquarters, and doubled his personal assistant's salary. One fatal flaw, though: They gave this Red X a telephone, which allowed him to stir up trouble from two zip codes away. Our guess is that the firm in question will be moving to choice E—Fire 'em—in the not-too-distant future. When firing them becomes the only viable solution, we often refer to the cartoon in Figure 6.1 as a way to frame the decision.

Figure 6.1

"Let's face it: you and this organization have never been a good fit."

Red Xs can fit well into other cultures. They are talented and can be repotted in different soil. Our advice to leaders who are firing someone—whether or not the person involved is a Red X—is to frame the event as a "good fit" discussion. This allows the leader to honestly support the Red X and to state sincerely, "We want you to be successful, and to be happy" ... but elsewhere. In FCG's experience, these decisions, though never easy, always work out better for all parties in the long run. Really.

Which leaves the final choice: *Fall in love with 'em.* This is where I always try to go. The Red Xs in this industry are quirky, egotistical, brilliant, and driven. Many of these clever people are absolutely fascinating. Spending time with them can be truly enjoyable. There are exceptions: I draw the line at Red Xs who are mean-spirited. I have not encountered many, but certainly there are some. They are poison to an organization. We know firms where one toxic Red X in a senior position can ruin the culture for everyone. (One Google leader writes, "Arrogant geniuses always backfire. They become a terror to other engineers. They may be a hundred times cleverer, but an arrogant genius can demoralize a thousand people."[86])

The *Fall in love with 'em* strategy involves a spiritual dimension. It asks us to expand our consciousness beyond what we label "comfortable." It has a "love thine enemy" quality to it. But humans are hard-wired to see *different* as *dangerous.* So, when we encounter a quirky and unorthodox Red X we instinctively get defensive. Especially if they are challenging our thinking. And especially, especially if they are challenging and correct!

In that case, we feel very defensive, like we are under attack. Our instinct is to expel the foreign object. So, the question in these cases is: "Can the culture stretch to absorb a benign Red X, or is it too disruptive?" We've seen situations like this go both ways: absorb or reject. Many times the absorb decision has paid off well for the firm. Again, for me the key factors to consider are arrogance (a complete lack of humility and curiosity) and mean-spiritedness (a perverse desire to belittle or bully others; see *The No Asshole Rule*[87] by Robert Sutton, PhD, for more on this). If either quality is present, then absorbing the Red X into the culture is a bad idea.

So, you have a bona fide Red X on staff, or have absorbed a new one. How do you lead this person? Let's return to our guest experts (Goffee and Jones, "Gojo") and see what they recommend. First off, they clearly state: "Our research suggests that leading clever people requires a very different style of leadership from that traditionally seen in many organizations."[88] In short, it requires both humility and toughness. Either alone is insufficient. In addition, Gojo emphasize a term they coined called "situation sensing." This means the ability "to tune in to their context: to view the world through their eyes … . [Such leaders] pick up and interpret soft data—sometimes without any verbal explanation. For example, they sense when a team is on task and on target or when additional resources are required."

Getting practical, Table 6.3 is a nice list of do's and don'ts for leading clever people, courtesy of Gojo.

Table 6.3 Leading Clever People

Do List	Don't List	FCG Comment
Explain and persuade	Tell people what to do	Telling clever people what to do implies that they are not smart, so they hate it. If you have to say "no" to them, then be sure to provide an explanation. Gojo say, "In the clever economy, command and control is ancient history." We know one CEO who regularly gets frustrated and gives orders to his Red Xs. This move always backfires.
Use expertise	Use hierarchy	In short, don't pull rank on clever people. One reason why investment people believe they can only be led by other investment people is the "expertise" argument. It goes like this: I'll respect you and possibly even follow you, if you are an expert (like me). Otherwise, forget it." Knowing the language of investments and markets allows you to speak the language of your clever people. VERY valuable.
Give people space and resources	Allow them to burn out	Give them the space and resources so that they use their brilliance constructively, rather than in a destructive pursuit of what they think they need. Gojo write, "[O]nce given the space and resources, there is rarely a need to motivate them. In fact, the opposite is the case. Leaders must ensure that their clever people aren't burned out by their obsessions." Work/life balance is a strong value in many investment firms.

Tell them what	Tell them how	Grand visions may be a distraction, whereas a sense of direction that unifies efforts is helpful. Importantly, "clever people are not only capable of figuring how to get something done, but they also take great pride in figuring out how to get it done *their* way."[89]
Provide boundaries	Create bureaucracy	Structure is important. Yes, give your clever people space, but also focus their efforts by providing some rules and discipline. Gojo suggest that a one-line summary for advice to leaders is: give them the environment that enables them to succeed. Give them "organized space." Eliminate anything that smacks of bureaucracy.
Give people time for questioning	Interfere	Even though clevers can be intellectually intimidating, Gojo recommend that CEOs be willing to engage them in debate. "Clevers tend to admire that intellectual engagement, some would say confrontation." Give clevers time to air their concerns, worries, and aspirations. Experiment with different communication channels. One size does not fit all.
Give recognition and amplify achievements	Give lots of feedback	Remember: clevers identify with their work, so recognizing their achievements is vital to their self-esteem (though most will deny it). The model that FCG uses for feedback is called ACE: Appreciation, Coaching, and Evaluation. Gojo suggest that the "A" should be used more than the "C" (providing tips) or the "E" (providing assessments of how they are doing). Most clevers do need stroking, but it has to be genuine and from someone they respect.
Encourage failure, maximize learning	Train	Ouch. FCG does a fair amount of training with investment people, so we looked hard at this one. Gojo put it this way: "[C]lever people view conventional training with disdain and as interference with their work. They learn best when faced with the next difficult assignment with an important client." In the case of investment professionals, they often get powerful lessons from post-mortems, analyzing their failures and successes. FCG estimates that only 10% of investment firms get valuable learnings from their experience. The training that we now do with investment firms is very practical and undertaken only after we've done careful prep work to "surface the need" (so that the training addresses it).
Protect clever people from the rain	Expose them to politics	One investment president describes his role as removing obstacles so that the investment pros can focus exclusively on their work. His bonus was based on how well he accomplished that goal. In exchange for "protection from the rain," we know investment professionals who would consider a cut in pay. Uninterrupted work time is that important.
Give real-world challenges with constraints	Build an ivory tower	This one applies more to academics, programmers, medical researchers, etc. But we have seen quant shops and even some fundamental investment shops which have enjoyed enough success to become insulated from performance. Most clever people are at their best when faced with "real and hard questions that they must solve within meaningful constraints." Conversely, every good investor we know is harder on himself/herself than any boss could be. The "piling on" doesn't help.
Talk straight	Bullshit	Investment clevers are both smart and skeptical, so they have excellent BS detectors. We advise investment leaders weekly to talk straight and be transparent—not only because it is the morally right thing to do, but also because, frankly, it is just stupid to do otherwise. Your clevers will see through the BS and learn the "secrets" anyway, so get out in front of it. Gojo put it this way: "Clevers typically have [an] uneasy relationship with firms which makes them supersensitive to perceived deceit, corporate speak, double-dealing, or any other strategy that implies they can be easily duped." They can't be.

Create a galaxy	Recruit a star	Gojo: "While it is conventional wisdom to seek to attract stars to an organization, the real leadership task is to ensure that these stars are connected to each other in ways that influence the entire organization. The leader is building a social architecture of knowledge. It's akin to using the best players on our soccer team to set the standards for everyone."[90] The good news for investment leaders is that clever people do not have to be Red Xs (i.e. difficult to work with). Some are, but others are brilliant and positive culture influencers.

Google is an organization that is often held up as very progressive, with lots of clevers. So, how do their leaders describe their roles? "We aim to offer people the freedom to be really good. I think that's what Google is really about: the freedom to do your best work. My job is to help make that happen."[91] Certainly this same statement applies to investment leaders. It is a talent business, and underneath all the scorn that clevers have for leadership, they "do want leadership from someone they respect."[92] They know that good leadership will result in a better work environment. Some structure is necessary.

Another Google leader sums it up this way: "The twentieth century was all about hardworking engineers. The twenty-first century is about flat organizations that must collaborate and compete."[93] As it relates to investment organizations, Kai-Fu Lee at Google has some interesting advice: "[T]he future needs to include not analysts but synthesizers. Clever organizations place a premium on the ability to synthesize multiple points of view. [Global macro funds, asset allocators?] Analysis only gets you so far. In the end, the clever economy requires synthesis: a recombining of inputs to create something new and better."[94]

How does this leadership discussion extend to culture management of clever firms? The glue for clever organization, according to Gojo, consists of four parts:

1. **Discipline:** Provide clear and simple rules. Two guidelines here: Have only a few rules, and make sure the rules are agreed upon. (The core values for the investment world are: client-centric, integrity, teamwork, and professional excellence.)
2. **Meaning (or, as Dan Pink calls it in *Drive*, "Purpose"):** One CEO puts it this way: "Clever people want to work with people they respect, doing meaningful things in a company that is respected externally." The Focus Elite—nine investment firms that we've referred to in this book—certainly meet these criteria.
3. **Trust:** No structural arrangement can work without the underpinning of widespread trust. Good communication stems from and supports trust.

4. **Genuine caring:** About both the clevers and the organization. *Passion* is a word we hear often in rooms with investment professionals. Despite all the lip service given to "objective, fact based" decision making, the truth is that conviction still rules the day. PMs want the analysts to promote stock ideas with real conviction; that is, passion. And investment professionals want their leaders to show this same passion for being a premier organization.

Gojo summarize their findings in this way:

Clear and simple rules, shared meaning, continuous dialogue (supported by trust), and really caring—this sounds like the stuff of a clever HR strategy.

Cleverness is not some sort of elixir of life. But the curiosity that is fundamental to cleverness is the essential lifeblood of the modern organization. Understanding, organizing, leading, and maximizing this is a great challenge. In the clever economy, only the curious will thrive. Any questions?[95]

Nice to see that Gojo emphasize the value of curiosity in their closing summary. As most of you know, curiosity is one of the core four behaviors—along with candor, appreciation, and accountability—that support all the other leadership skillsets.

Speaking of accountability, we'll go there next. Accountability is the number 1 antidote to bad behavior, even that of Red Xs. So read on for understanding the right way to do it.

---

[81] Rob Goffee and Gareth Jones, *Clever: Leading Your Smartest, Most Creative People* (Harvard Business Press, 2009), https://www.amazon.com/Clever-Leading-Smartest-Creative-People-ebook/dp/B005DI8XQC/ref=sr_1_2?ie=UTF8&qid=1526051243&sr=8-2&keywords=leading+clever+people

[82] *Ibid.*, p. 45.

[83] *Ibid.*, p. 178.

[84] *Ibid.*, p. 123.

[85] *Ibid.*, p. 57.

[86] *Ibid.*, p. 189.

[87] Robert Sutton, *The No Asshole Rule: Building a Civilized Workplace and Surviving One That Isn't* (Business Plus, 2007), https://www.amazon.com/Asshole-Rule-Civilized-Workplace-Surviving-ebook/dp/B000OT8GV2/ref=sr_1_1?s=digital-text&ie=UTF8&qid=1526052756&sr=1-1&keywords=the+no+asshole+rule.

[88] Goffee and Jones, *Clever.*

[89] *Ibid.*, p. 211.

[90] *Ibid.*, p. 68.

[91] *Ibid.*, p. 50.

[92] *Ibid.*, p. 51.

[93] *Ibid.*, p. 51.

[94] *Ibid.*, p. 52.

[95] *Ibid.*, p. 201.

CHAPTER 7

Accountability: Defining It and Executing on It

Many investment firms are taking the sucker's bet on accountability. Is yours? Let's define the sucker's bet: It's an either/or choice in which both options are bad ones. (It's a bit like, "Have you stopped beating your spouse?" Either answer condemns you.) The good news with accountability is that a wise choice does exist. Unfortunately, many firms don't see it.

Accountability is a core value for investment firms. We know this from our survey work. Often it is subsumed under "integrity" or "professional[ism]," but it always rises to the top of the "must have" values. Accountability is linked to fairness. If people are falling short of their goals or shirking their duties altogether, then it seems unfair to let them off the hook (i.e., *not* hold them accountable). In the ideal firm, each person knows her or his role and goals and takes responsibility for fulfilling them.

Recently FCG has worked with three excellent investment firms, all with good track records and known brands. In each case, we asked the leaders of the firms, "What values would help eliminate sludge and improve results for the firm?" We showed them a list of the most common values at investment firms and asked them to vote (using clickers). Table 7.1 shows the vote from one firm with its 50 leaders.

Table 7.1 Sludge-Reduction Behaviors

Which behaviors/attitudes below would help to reduce this firm's sludge? (pick 3)	
More accountability	28%
More trust	23%
More respect	21%
More excellence	19%
More clarity and precision	9%

Sure enough, accountability is the top vote-getter at 28%. In FCG's experience, values fall into one of two broad categories, "tough love" or "TLC: Tender Loving Care." In other words, some values represent the tough side of leadership, such as holding people accountable, or pushing for more excellence. Others represent the supportive side of leadership, such as caring and listening. In our crayon-simple way, FCG has labeled these sets of values the "fist" and the "open hand." A sample list is shown in Table 7.2.

Table 7.2 Two-Handed Leadership

Open Hand	Closed Fist
Listening	Discipline
Appreciation	Accountability
Caring	Clarity
Respect	Directing
Forgiveness	Excellence/demanding
Safety	Candor
Feedback: encouraging	Feedback:critical
Trust: caring	Trust: competency
Focus on process	Focus on results

In our view, good leaders understand and practice both sides of this chart. Leadership is situational. Sometimes staff members need to feel supported, other times they need a push. Good leaders know when to use each.

So, what is the vote in Table 7.2 telling us? (And remember, this result was nearly identical for three different firms.) Add up the "fist" votes and the "open hand" votes and you get more fist than open hand. And yet culture data clearly shows that all of these firms operate in much more "open hand" fashion. So, why is there a disconnect between what these leaders know that they need and what they have?

Back to the sucker's choice. Why don't these firms simply turn up the volume on the "fist" to achieve the proper balance between fist and open hand? A comment from a participant captured the sucker's choice nicely. He said, "So what you are telling us is that we can offer the candy bar in the open hand, or the whip in the closed fist?" Bingo. There's the sucker's choice. To put it in cultural terms: we can be a nice place to work, where people are polite and civil—with no accountability—or we can be an abusive sweatshop where people get lashings when they don't perform. That's the sucker's choice. The nice place to work has little accountability and operates suboptimally, whereas the "fist" shop whips people into shape but is a nasty place to work.

What's the solution? It requires a reframing of what it means to use the fist. In fact, the fist is not whipping people. It's a culture in which the values of precision, discipline, excellence, and candor are understood and practiced. Instead of a whip, picture the fist holding a scalpel. (No! Not for slicing up people!) The scalpel represents surgical precision. Most firms use butter knives, which make for sloppy agreements, fuzzy roles, and blurry decision rights. The surgical scalpel is used to make precise agreements, specific roles, and clear decision rights. An example? After a lengthy discussion, a leader says, "Okay, will one of you follow up on this as soon as possible?" Everyone nods. (It would be rude to do otherwise.) This approach is the butter knife: imprecise and fuzzy. The scalpel approach is different. It follows the "Who will do what by when?" formula, and it sounds like this: "Sarah, will you summarize this discussion on one page with a recommendation at the bottom and send it around to us by 5 pm tomorrow?" The candor part of the fist leadership is when Sarah responds, "I have three client meetings between now and tomorrow at 5 pm, so unless you want me to reschedule one of them, I am not available to do it." Notice: No one is getting whipped or sliced open, but they are operating with precision and candor.

Far too many firms consider this fist approach to be rude. Again, that's the sucker's choice: "We can be a nice place to work with decent people (and we get candy), or a rude place with hostile people." Wrong. You can be a very nice place to work that also takes seriously the values of: accountability, precision, candor, and clarity.

So, how could you as a leader move your team or firm in this direction? You first identify and agree on the problem: We are out of balance. We are too much the open hand rather than the closed fist. (Like 12-step programs: "My name is John and I'm a recovering open-hand leader.") Then you start to leverage the open-hand values, like appreciation and respect, to highlight and promote the fist values. How? By putting your attention on the examples within the firm that demonstrate good fist behavior. When someone makes a very clear agreement, you acknowledge them publicly: "John, I want to appreciate you for that clear agreement you just made. The 'who, what, and when' were all identified with precision." Or, on the accountability front, you recognize a team member for giving direct feedback about a missed deadline. It might sound like this: "I'm aware that we made an agreement to have the RFP ready for this meeting, so we could review it. The proposal is not ready. I'm curious. What happened?" Again, no whipping, no blaming, but clarity around the missed deadline, and curiosity around why it was missed. In these conversations, watch for the appearance of victims, villains, and heroes. They sound like this:

Victim: "I wasn't given enough time to finish the RFP. And no one gave me any help. I was left to do it all by myself." (Poor me)

Villain: "Why did you accept the assignment if you knew damn well you weren't going to get it done? How do you expect to raise our accountability if you keep acting like this?" (It's your fault, you idiot)

Hero: "I know you gave it your best shot. We're all busy, and sometimes things fall through the cracks. I'll give you another day, and I'll help you get it done." (Let him off the hook; I'll do it. And in doing so, I will look like a saint!)

These behaviors are common in cultures dominated by the open hand. They reflect the fact that no one is taking 100% responsibility for the work. The villains and victims each take 0%: they blame others or the circumstances. The hero takes 200% responsibility, covering for others and taking up the slack. A culture that properly balances the fist and the open hand sees less and less of these behaviors and much more candid and clear conversations about accountability. A move toward the fist is a move toward a more mature and courageous culture.

So, there is a way to balance the fist with the open hand. Remember, a move toward more accountability does not mean that the culture must become nasty or mean-spirited. Rather, a move toward accountability is a move towards clarity, precision, candor, and excellence. FCG recommends that you talk about this shift openly. Explain to the team what you are trying to do: create a culture of accountability. This goal requires a balancing of the two forces: the fist and open hand. Research on great leaders indicates that they practice two fist traits (integrity and responsibility) and two open-hand traits (compassion and forgiveness). That is the goal of strong leaders. Have both tools in your kit and know when to use each.

Three important tools must be sharpened if you wish to become a truly accountable organization.

1. Roles and responsibilities must be clear.
2. The goals for each role must be negotiated and agreed on.
3. Feedback must be used to close any gaps. Skillful delivery and receipt of feedback is necessary to close accountability gaps.

In one firm, a senior PM told us, "I've stopped giving candid feedback because when I do it shows up in my year-end review as being hostile. I get docked in my bonus for not being a team player." Here again is the sucker's choice: polite (but suboptimal) vs. rude (but more effective). Good leaders will not take the sucker's choice of either/or. Instead, they will opt for both/and. We can be a great place to work with genuinely good and caring people AND create a culture of accountability through practicing candor, precision, and excellence. We can choose the fist AND the open hand.

All right, now the hard part. You've explained the basic concept of accountability to your team:

1. Get a clear agreement up front about the deliverable. Both of you should be clear about what is expected. Have a metric in place to show success or failure.
2. Monitor the employee's progress. If all goes well, appreciate them. If course corrections are needed, provide feedback. (Use the cube that we described earlier.)
3. Appreciate the final success, or do a post mortem if there is failure.

Let's look at the final piece of this list: post-mortem a failure. Basically, failure means a broken agreement. The project was moving along well, you had monitored progress, all seemed good for a successful finish. But instead, the person drops the ball and fails. (Most of these failures occur because implementation of steps 1 and 2 was sloppy: the agreement is not clear, and no real monitoring happens. Often these broken agreements occur across departments: a salesperson expects a PM to go with her to visit a big client, but the PM claims he never knew about the meeting, or bows out at the last minute.) Visually, accountability gaps look like Figure 7.1.

Figure 7.1 Accountability Gaps

Now you are facing the tough part of accountability: dealing with these broken agreements. You feel disappointed, maybe a little angry as well. Lawyers call these incidents breaches of contract. At work we may call them gaps or missed commitments. Now you face a crucial confrontation.[96] Most of us would rather have a root canal with no anesthesia than have this conversation. Why? Because we've never really learned *how* to have such conversations. We know we're going into dangerous territory without equipment, training, or backup. Gulp. So, we try to finesse it. In the history of business, this has worked three times. (Okay, I'm exaggerating. It's worked seventeen times ...)

Don't despair. There is a way to handle these conversations skillfully. You don't need to pray for divine intervention. The following set of steps will help you address and resolve the toughest part of accountability: the big, nasty, undeniably broken agreement.

Step 1: Determine **WHAT** the problem is. Example: Your co-PM on the portfolio shows up 15 minutes late for the 9:00 am meeting with analysts. If this is the first and only time that your co-PM has shown up late, then you can nip it in the bud by addressing it as a one-off. You might appreciate him for his normal punctuality and ask if everything is all right, given this one instance of being late. Fine. But, what if it happens a second and third time? Now a pattern is developing. So, it's useful to think of:

- **Consequences:** What are the business consequences of the behavior?
- **Intentions:** What is your story about why the co-PM comes late to meetings?

By considering both consequences and intentions regarding repeated violations, you can get a clearer statement of what you believe is the real problem. It's important to be able to state concisely what your concern is: *"When you come late to our weekly meetings, it sends a message that you don't value the analysts' input. My story is that this hurts team morale."*

Step 2: Determine **IF** you should raise the issue. Not every broken agreement is worth a crucial conversation. After you've done step 1—concisely identified the real issue—then you still must decide if you want to bring it up. In this regard, there are three useful questions to ask yourself:

1. Is your **conscience nagging** you? You tell yourself it's no big deal, but your gut tells you that you should say something. Pay attention to that voice. Use FCG's "rule of three." If your conscience nags you three times, you should probably say something.
2. Are you **rationalizing**? Are you downplaying the significance of the issue because it will be hard to deal with? Get past the question of "Will it be difficult" and ask yourself, "Should it be done?"
3. Are you **playing victim** (helpless)? You tell yourself that there's nothing you can do to improve the situation. You don't have the skills to approach the other person. But even a small degree of skill in the steps described in this chapter can help considerably.

Finally, if you are operating in a culture that hasn't taken accountability too seriously in the past, then it behooves you to "call your shot." Don't just spring this higher, more demanding level of accountability on the team, though; give them fair warning. Reset their expectations—and do it in a way that doesn't look smug. Be respectful. You may want to say, "I know there are parts of this organization that are informal about accountability, but I think it will serve us well to get better at it. I believe we can raise our game by being more precise around accountability." (This approach works much better than labeling people incompetent cowards.)

Step 3: Come from a **POSITIVE INTENTION**. Check in with yourself about why you are giving the feedback. Make sure you're not viewing this conversation as a chance to get revenge. That never goes well. A useful way to review what you are going to say is to cube it, a method we introduced earlier but merits repeating (Figure 7.2).

Figure 7.2 Trust Cube

FACTS		STORY
• Prior agreements • Actions • Results • Video camera view	**+**	• Opinions • Judgments • Interpretation • Assumptions

REQUEST		REACTION
• Request • Action Plan • Development • Improved skill or knowledge	**=**	• Gratitude • Anger • Disappointment • Fear • Excitement

- Start by assembling your **facts**. What is unarguable about the situation? (For example, that your co-PM was late for three meetings. It's helpful to be able to state specifically what times the PM arrived.)
- Then ask yourself, "What **story** do I make up about the facts?" (For example, that the co-PM does not respect you or the team.) Remember to "hold your story lightly," because it may be wrong! Be careful of assigning a label to the person: "slacker" or "arrogant." It's highly unlikely that the other person sees himself this way! And, what is the business impact of your story?
- Consider your **reaction**. Are you worried? Concerned? Angry? Keep in mind that your story is creating your reaction! (What if the co-PM was told by the CEO to show up late so that you could set the tone for the meetings? That fact might well create a completely different story and reaction.)
- Finally, decide what you want. What is your **request**? What change do you want to see in the future and why?

After you've played with this cubing-it exercise, ask yourself if you are giving the other person the benefit of the doubt (i.e., assuming good intentions). A good question to ask yourself is: Why would an intelligent and decent person act this way? (If you find yourself re-wording this question to "Why does this bastard have to be such a jerk?" then you have a bit more preparation work to do.)

Step 4: SAFELY DESCRIBE the gap. So far, you haven't said anything to the other person. You've thought through the situation and defined the issue, asked yourself if you should bring it up, and then checked out your intention (is it positive)? Finally, you've played with cubing the situation, so as to clearly understand where you are coming from and what you want. Now, you're ready to speak. The first words out of your mouth are critically important. Remember our old friend, the amygdala? The lizard part of your brain is watching for anything that might be dangerous. So, if you start the conversation with an accusation—boom!—the amygdala will hijack the rational part of your counterpart's brain and prepare her for fight or flight. She may not actually start hyperventilating, but I can assure you she is not hearing a word you are saying. And if she is, it probably sounds to her like, "I know where you live and how to wire a car bomb."

So, what's the secret to success? Start with *safety*. People feel unsafe when they believe one of two things:

1. You don't respect them as a human being. (You lack **mutual respect**)
2. You don't share a mutual goal. You have competing agendas. (You lack **mutual purpose**)

Therefore, establish mutual respect and purpose. Explain that your intentions are positive and find an outcome you can both agree on: happy client, excellent report, strong team, top results, whatever. You want to solve the problem and you want to make things better. If you sense that the other person is already becoming defensive, then use a technique called "contrasting." Identify his fear—loss of job, reduced bonus, no promotion, and so on—and directly address it.[97] It may sound like this:

> *"I suspect that you might be worried that this situation affects your chances for a promotion, but I assure you that is NOT what this conversation is about. You are highly valued. I just want to discuss the Smith account, understand what went wrong in our last meeting, and brainstorm how we can make things better."*

Obviously, you have to be sincere in this statement. It never, ever pays to mislead someone. Be sincere, but also be direct. (Don't be like the CEO who was instructed to be sincere and responded, "No problem, I can fake that.") Don't insult someone by playing games or hinting or challenging them to read your mind. Establish safety, then describe the gap.

To continue with our co-PM example, you might simply say to your colleague, "I noticed that you came late to the last few team meetings. I was wondering what happened. Is there something I should know about or can help with?" If your co-PM doesn't get defensive and seems quite willing to rationally discuss the situation, then fine. Watch for defensiveness, though. At the slightest sign of it, forget about the issue (the "content") and re-establish safety (the "process"). You are walking a parallel path in these confrontations: content and process, the message and safety. When safety seems threatened, step out of content and rebuild safety. Safety first, always.

As in the preceding example, end with a question. Show sincere curiosity. Describe the gap and then ask an open-ended question, like, "Help me understand …?"

Step 5: DIAGNOSE will or skill. After you have safely described the gap (e.g., shortfall in performance, or broken agreement), and asked an open-ended question, get curious about the person's will or skill. Is the person unmotivated? Or is the person unable to do the task? In short, your job as manager—or as peer—is to help bring out the best in your teammates. So, when a colleague or colleagues are failing at a task, your two big levers are:

1. **Make it motivating**. Help them want to do it. Help them understand the consequences of their failure and link it to something they care about. See if you

can reach a place where they are genuinely motivated. A personal example: My wife is not a "money person." She just doesn't care about making a big income. But she does care deeply about animal causes. When she links making more money to making bigger donations to animal causes, she gets excited about more income (and encourages me to do the same).

2. **Make it easy**. Act not by bullying or hero-ing (micromanaging), but by being an expert enabler: one who can make the job easier for them. (Sometimes that means teaching them what the job is.) For those of us who are puritanical by nature, this can mean letting go of the idea that something must be difficult and noxious for it to be valuable. It's okay to look for an easier, more efficient way to accomplish the task. This might mean brainstorming ways to remove barriers. Play Socrates. Ask good questions. Let them solve the issue. Avoid being the hero who rushes in to save the day. Ask them for their ideas. Get genuinely curious about their ability to solve it on their own. Listen and encourage. And avoid the two common mistakes:

   a. **Leading the witness**: Pretending to listen but really just guiding them to your solution.

   b. Playing **Mr. Know-it-all**: Having an answer to any question they pose, even when you have no clue!

Finally, a wonderful question to ask is, "If you were CEO, what would you do to solve this problem?" Giving the person this new framework can often unleash very creative ideas about how to eliminate barriers. Challenge the status quo. Many policies and procedures are outdated and should be reworked.

Step 6: DEVELOP a plan. So far you have safely described the gap in performance, diagnosed whether the cause is will (motivation) or skill (ability), and brainstormed a new approach that seems like a workable solution. Great. The final step is to clearly set out the plan for follow-up. Make sure that before you exhaust yourself with self-congratulatory NFL end-zone dances, you have a "who will do what by when" statement—and a plan for monitoring and following up.

There you have it: a six-step plan for addressing broken promises, missed deadlines, performance gaps. A fair question at this point is, "But what if you get sidetracked?" You think you are addressing a missed deadline and suddenly it becomes evident that your employee has lied to you on several other occasions. Be clear. If a separate issue comes up, name it: "honesty." Then decide which is more important: the missed deadline, or the trust issue with your subordinate? You can use the same six-step process on the new issue. Just be clear and don't meander. Consciously choose the most important issue and then stick with it.

As with any skill, practice makes perfect … or at least helps. Don't expect to get this process exactly right the first time you use it. But trust me on this, it does get easier. And you will get better at it.

So, as you take aim at improved accountability for your team and your firm, remember the Triple A formula:

1. Clear **Agreements**. What are you holding them accountable for? And do they buy in?
2. **Acceptance** of responsibility. All staff members take responsibility for their contribution to the results; they don't hide or blame others. They are also open to feedback which allows for good monitoring and course correction when necessary.
3. **Achievement**. When goals are achieved, managers appreciate the team members and set new goals. When goals are missed, managers follow the six-step process to discover what went wrong and how to fix it.

Let's end on a positive note. If you and your team mates embrace the goal of becoming more accountable and have even modest success, you will be way ahead of the typical firm. So, in this ever more competitive landscape, accountability is clearly a place where you can gain an edge. And isn't that nice to consider?

Okay, if you are still reading, then clearly you are motivated to be a good leader. Wonderful. The industry sorely needs you. The next chapter is arguably the most important of all: emotional intelligence (EQ). We touched on it earlier, but now we'll take a deeper dive. People with low EQ will never be great leaders. You must know yourself, read your team members accurately, and be able to combine these skills to manage effectively.

The problem, of course, is that people with low EQ don't know they have low EQ … Read on to improve yours.

---

[96] This term is from the best book we know on the topic: *Crucial Confrontations: Tools for Talking When Stakes Are High* by Kerry Patterson, Joseph Grenny, Rob McMillan, and Al Switzler (McGraw-Hill, 2005).

[97] FCG has found that people usually get defensive because they fear the loss of 1) security, 2) approval, or 3) control. A feedback approach that acknowledges these three major fears and does not threaten or trigger them is optimal.

CHAPTER 8

Emotional Intelligence: Becoming People Smart

E arlier we mentioned emotional intelligence (EQ) and described it briefly. It merits a deeper look for two reasons:

1. Evidence suggests that it is one of the most important factors linked to success.
2. In FCG's 360 reviews of investment pros, it is the weakest skill.

Warren Buffett's view of EQ is: "If you have a 150 I.Q., sell 30 points to someone else. You need to be smart, but not a genius."[98] Rather, Buffett famously says that the most valuable factor for successful investors is temperament. That's code for EQ.

Unsurprisingly, many investment professionals resist the "soft stuff." Many prefer a bout of Montezuma's revenge to a discussion of emotional intelligence. At offsites, EQ provokes predictable responses: eye-rolling, finger tapping, cavernous yawning, and wristwatch glancing. I feel as welcome as Jack Bogle at a hedge fund conference.

Though predictable, this response is counterproductive. The research is clear: IQ gets you in the door, but EQ gets you to the winner's circle. Because many readers are data

driven, I want to present some findings from our 360 database. We've done hundreds of 360 reviews on investment leaders around the globe. The process involves a participant being assessed by direct reports, peers, and bosses (hence the term *360*). The assessment contains both objective scores on various competencies—strategic thinking, effective decision making, client focus—and written comments on a participant's strengths and weaknesses. (Each 360 assessment contains 20—25 competencies from three leadership categories: leads the self, leads the team, and leads the firm.)

My hypothesis going into the analysis on EQ was that self-awareness would be a key factor in overall scoring. Specifically, if a person demonstrated high self-awareness, then his overall score, for all the competencies measured, would be high. Conversely, those with low self-awareness would do "poorly" on their 360.

The data confirmed this hypothesis. We ran a correlation to look at the relationship strength between total average score and the competencies. The two competencies showing the strongest positive correlation to total average score were:

1. Provides Direction ($r = .88$)
2. Self-awareness ($r = .87$)

The top competency, "Provides Direction," squares with our earlier assertion that "Clear Purpose and Direction" is the number-one factor in explaining team success. Great leaders—with high 360 results—understand that providing clear direction is crucial to team performance. Makes sense.

But right behind "Provides Direction" was the variable in question: self-awareness. In our 360, *self-awareness* is defined as:

- Knows one's own strengths and weaknesses
- Seeks feedback and attempts to always learn and improve themselves
- Consistently practices self-reflection

The results of our analysis confirmed our hypothesis: individuals who score highly on these measures also tend to score highest on overall 360 results. Additionally, we found a strong positive correlation between self-awareness and the following three competencies:

- Reading people ($r = .77$)
- Builds effective collaboration ($r = .80$)
- Integrity and trust ($r = .77$)

Self-awareness is the starting point. It drives the other EQ competencies. Further, self-awareness—and emotional intelligence (all four boxes)—seems to drive success in the remaining 360 competencies as well. Remember, IQ gets you in the door, but EQ gives you the competitive advantage. Looking at the difference between the top scorers on the 360s and the bottom ones, we see a significant difference in self-awareness scores (1 to 5 scale with 5 as top score) (Tables 8.1A–E).

Table 8.1A

Top 360 scores: average self-awareness score	**4.24**
Bottom 360 scores: average self-awareness score	**3.08**

Let's look at a real example. Consider two investment pros from the same firm. They each participated in a 360 review with the same group of raters (apples-to-apples comparison). The results confirmed that each one is seen as a gifted investor, and highly regarded for his technical skills. In addition, my interviews with their raters revealed that each one is a good person, with good intentions. In short, neither is a Red X (i.e., a jerk).

Interestingly, when we move away from technical skills and IQ, their 360 results are very different. One had a high overall average (4.6), the other low (3.3). Looking at our hypothesis—that self-awareness will determine overall competency scores—we see it confirmed in these self-awareness scores.

Table 8.1B

	High scorer on 360	Low scorer on 360
Self-assessment on self- awareness	4.0	3.5
Peer assessment on self-awareness	4.4	2.5

Digging a bit deeper into these self-awareness scores, one of the questions on self-awareness reads, "I seek feedback and attempt to always learn and improve myself." This question captures a key competency studied by the Center for Creative Leadership (Greensborough, NC), which they call "Learning Agility." Basically, Learning Agility means that a person is open and receptive to feedback and makes good use of it. CCL's research found that this competency was the primary determinant of executive success. Table 8.1C shows each person's score on Learning Agility.

Table 8.1C

	High scorer on 360	Low scorer on 360
Self-assessment on seeks feedback, committed to learning and improving	5.0	4.0
Peer assessment on seeks feedback, committed to learning and improving	4.9	2.1

The results for these two individuals are a microcosm of what we found overall. Good leadership skills depend on high self-awareness. When I debrief 360 results with individuals, I can tell pretty quickly if they are open to learning and improving. High self-awareness scorers lean in to the results. They pay attention. They ask questions. They want to improve.

Unfortunately, many low self-awareness scorers have the opposite reaction. One case in particular, described earlier in this book, stands out. Remember the PM who resisted the whole 360 process? He was so convinced that the results would be biased that he requested two different sets of raters: one that he picked, and one that was picked at random. He was quite sure that the two rating groups would show markedly different results. (In the process, the PM did not fill out his self-assessment.) In fact, the two groups were similar, and both groups scored the PM poorly. The results are shown in Table 8.1D.

Table 8.1D

	Self-assessment scores	Peer assessment scores
Self-awareness (overall)	(did not complete)	2.3
Seeks feedback, attempts to learn and improve	(did not complete)	2.0

When it came time to review the 360 results with me, it was evident that this PM had not read the report. In our debrief, he spent most of the time asking questions that were unrelated to his 360. In fact, we never did open the report and review it. Afterward, he refused any follow-up coaching, and to this day I'm quite sure he has never reviewed the report. This firm loses analysts on a regular basis because they don't want to work with this PM. (At last count, the firm had lost nearly 50 analysts over a 5-year period.)

My reaction to experiences like this is both sadness and compassion. I would like to see all people learn and improve. These individuals who have low EQs are not bad people.

In fact, they are good people with great technical skills. No question, they could learn and improve. Unfortunately, they choose to be defensive and closed, rather than curious and open.

The good news is that some of them "get it." The light turns on. They see that their defensive stance is harmful to reaching full potential. Over time, they do open up and begin to learn. A success story in this regard involves a COO who initially showed all the resistant, defensive signs. He challenged our process, our credentials, and our motives ("consultants just want to find weaknesses so they can get hired"). When he saw the results, he questioned them as well. They were poor. Table 8.1E shows this COO's scores on self-awareness and learning agility.

Table 8.1E

	Self-assessment scores	Peer assessment scores
Self-awareness (overall)	4.7	3.1
Seeks feedback, attempts to learn and improve	4.0	2.9

The turning point for the COO occurred when we asked him to show the results to his family. We said, "If they agree that the results are bogus, then we won't ever mention the 360 again." He followed our suggestion. He showed the results to his wife and adult children and they responded nonchalantly: "Yes, that's you." The COO was shocked. He had no idea that he was affecting people this way. He decided then and there that he wanted to change his image. Several years have passed and he has become a model for collaboration, respect, and fairness. Colleagues of his have told us many times that the COO has changed remarkably for the better. Importantly, this COO was in his late fifties. Many of the 360 resisters use the excuse, "I'm too old to change," or the broader statement, "People don't change." They are wrong. People can and do change—but only if they are open to feedback and committed to learning.

The preceding story always encourages me to give every effort to coaching people who initially resist. People in this industry are exceptionally bright and basically good-natured. If they are willing to drop the Ego's goal of resisting change, then self-awareness and EQ can improve significantly. It's a choice. Some of my favorite coaching experiences involve individuals who made the choice to learn and change.

So far the message is clear: IQ (technical skill) opens the door, but EQ provides the competitive advantage. Drop your Ego defenses and learn all you can.

Here's a question for you. If you could spend a day with Warren Buffett or with Daniel Goleman, whom would you choose?

Warren Buffett, right?

I assume every reader would make this choice. I mean, who wouldn't want to sit at the feet of the Oracle of Omaha? Arguably the greatest investor of all time, and hugely entertaining as well. No brainer, right?

Wrong.

Why is it wrong to choose Buffett over Goleman? (I'm guessing many readers didn't even recognize the name "Daniel Goleman" before opening this book, although they may recognize his work on emotional intelligence.) Here's why. As investment experts, you're probably familiar with most of Buffett's wisdom. You've read his annual reports, maybe attended his annual "Woodstock-for-investors" meetings, and certainly seen the many books and articles about him. Is his reputation merited? For sure.

But choosing a day with Warren is wrong because, as we said earlier about his view, temperament, more than IQ or technical skills, is important to winning the investment game. And that's what EQ is all about: temperament. EQ is about how you manage your emotions, and how you leverage that skill to your benefit.

From FCG's extensive work with investment pros, we know that EQ is not their towering strength. In simple terms, they have massive IQ and modest EQ. Sometimes the gap is remarkable (think: *Sherlock Holmes, The Accountant, or House*). In some cases, this gap is acceptable. If a person is an individual contributor—say, an analyst or a strategist—then low EQ may be somewhat less damaging. Their role is to add value through doing their own work well, and—providing they don't create havoc—this works.

But for investment pros who must collaborate—especially in a team leader role—then EQ is vital. Table 8.1F is a simple model of EQ.

Table 8.1F

	What I see	What I do
Personal Competence	Self-awareness	Self-management
Social Competence	Social awareness	Relationship management

The model starts with Self-awareness: knowing your strengths and weaknesses, recognizing your thoughts and feelings, and having healthy self-esteem. Then the model moves to self-management: "Okay, I know myself pretty well, can I manage myself?" Do you have the temperament that Buffett refers to, or do you lose control, panic, become irrational, yell at colleagues, pout, and so on? A person with good self-awareness and good self-management appears calm, centered, and responsible (i.e., able to respond as appropriate). Then the model moves beyond the self to others: *social awareness*. Are you reading others well? Do you have a sense of the environment you're in? If you're leading a meeting, do you recognize that it's time for a break because people are fidgeting and looking at their watches?

These three skillsets—self-awareness, self-management, social awareness—are necessary for the final skillset: relationship management. This final skill is where it all comes together. If you've mastered the first three, you are now able to interact—and lead—effectively. You know yourself pretty well, you can manage yourself, and you read others well enough to act effectively on a team.

In FCG's 360 assessment work, we use the competencies in Table 8.2 to measure the four quadrants of EQ.

Table 8.2 Four Quadrants of EQ

Self-awareness	Self-management
• Knows own strengths and weaknesses • Seeks feedback and attempts to always learn and improve oneself • Consistently practices self-reflection	• Integrity and trust • Temperament • Self-motivated
Social awareness	**Relationship management**
• Has the ability to quickly identify strengths and weaknesses of others • Can accurately assess what an individual is like and how a person is likely to perform • Is keenly aware of the social environment and those in it • Understands why others act as they do • Understands what matters and what motivates others	• Builds effective collaboration • Provides direction • Develops others • Addresses and resolves conflict

In FCG's analysis of 360 data from investment pros, we indeed confirm that self-awareness is the starting point for EQ. The strong positive correlations between self-awareness and the other quadrants are as follows:

- Self-management (r = .77)
- Social awareness (r = .79)
- Relationship management (r = .80)

Goleman[99] makes this point clearly in his writings: EQ starts with self-awareness. If you are clueless about your own "operating system," then you won't be effective in the other quadrants. For example, if you don't recognize and understand why you get frustrated and angry easily, you won't understand why you're collaborating ineffectively. Specifically, you won't try to manage your anger (because you're not aware of it). Therefore, you won't appear appropriately calm and reasonable. And you won't notice that others are avoiding you (because you get angry at them). And you won't understand why your team is ineffective. Importantly, you won't receive vital feedback, which is the key to increasing self-awareness (because feedback helps identify blindspots). Therefore:

1. Step one for high EQ is self-awareness. Know your strengths and weaknesses. Be aware of your thoughts and feelings. Know what triggers you to behave badly. Get curious. Get feedback.
2. Step two is mastering the next two quadrants: self-management and social awareness. Self-management obviously requires self-awareness. You can't manage what you aren't aware of. But self-awareness is also important to social awareness. If you don't understand your own internal landscape, it's nearly impossible to recognize and understand that of others. You won't read people well. You don't read yourself well! As you begin to understand yourself, you begin to understand others better. Do we have proof that self-awareness drives these two other factors? Yes, our regression work indicates this relationship is accurate at the 99% confidence level.

Do these skillsets— self-management and social awareness—drive higher scores for relationship management? Yes. As Goleman predicts, self-awareness is necessary for high social awareness and self-management, and these two, in turn, determine relationship management:

Predicted Relationship Management Score =
0.62 (social awareness) + 0.84 (self-management) - 2.14

This regression is also significant at the 99% confidence level. These two variables explain over 80% of one's relationship management score.

Back to our original question: Buffett or Goleman? Most of you don't need more investment wisdom, and you mostly know what Buffett has to say. What would actually help your team's performance is more EQ.

A recent study of hedge fund managers supports this view that being "people smart" is an advantage:

> *In the world of high finance, it's been an article of faith among some that the only way to succeed—or even survive—is to be ruthless. But a new study in the latest issue of the Personality & Social Psychology Bulletin suggests those money makers at the top of the food chain, hedge fund managers, could benefit from being a little less mean. [They] actually perform worse than their peers over time … . Investing, like other fields, requires collaboration, listening to the ideas of colleagues, and hiring specialists to execute your strategies.*[100]

How does EQ benefit performance? Some examples include:

* Remaining calm in the midst of market chaos
* Creating a safe environment for trust, candor, and constructive debate
* Getting more feedback at all levels: boss, direct reports, and peers
* Managing behavioral biases, such as confirmation bias or hindsight bias
* Improving client relationships through better listening and understanding of their viewpoints

For these reasons and more, you now know the wiser choice between Buffett and Goleman. My guess? Most investors will still pick Buffett. It's just too darn tempting.

Congrats on staying the course. I sincerely hope that these ideas help you lead well. Your direct reports, clients, and owners will all appreciate it. Plus, you'll enjoy greater success and more personal satisfaction.

The essays that follow in Appendices A I are directed at certain topics that FCG gets asked about regularly.

---

[98] Warren Buffett

[99] For more on Goleman, see http://myframeworks.org/emotional-intelligence-experts/daniel-goleman/?gclid=EAIaIQobChMI246ss4iC1wIVg0OGCh39LQOIEAAYASAAEgIOTfD_BwE

[100] Ben Steverman, "Being Manipulative and Mean Isn't the Secret to Success, A New Study by Two Psychology Professors Says." https://twitter.com/bsteverman

Appendix A: Integrity: Defining It Beyond "Do the Right Thing"

Integrity is a core value of investment firms—as it should be—based on FCG's extensive culture work in the industry. More firms claim to be practicing integrity than any of the other common values: excellence, client satisfaction, teamwork, or accountability.

Here's the rub. Most investment professionals—including CEOs—have not thought carefully about integrity beyond the general notion of "do the right thing." Which is a fine start. The dirty little secret in the investment world is that most of us care more about markets and money than integrity. We can talk for hours about discounted cash flow, foreign exchange, passive vs. active, ETFs, DB and DC markets, and the like, but our discussion of integrity is limited to, um, "do the right thing." Even if people agreed about what that meant, studies show that average people only follow through on 3 of 10 promises (consider New Year's resolutions). Not a good score for integrity.

Brace yourself. I'll try to make this entertaining, but the topic isn't exactly lighthearted.

Enter Werner Erhard (EST and Landmark Forum) and Michael Jensen (Harvard professor and founder of Social Science Research Network [SSRN]). In their paper, "Putting Integrity into Finance: A Purely Positive Approach,"[101] they go into great depth and detail

I only cheated a little.

about the importance and definition of integrity. In the first place, they elevate integrity to a factor of production. In their view, integrity is a necessary ingredient to business success, as important as labor, capital, or resources. This view opposes the more common one: integrity exists as a virtue (or ideal) rather than as a necessary condition of performance. They call integrity a necessary but *not* sufficient factor in creating long-run value maximization. A key term they use is "workability," which means "capable of producing the desired effect or result." The causal link in the paper is as follows: integrity => workability => performance => long-run value. In short, no integrity, no long-run value. The authors believe that their claim "long-run value maximization requires integrity" is a positive proposition that is testable and refutable. I would use simpler language: high integrity leads to high performance; conversely, low integrity leads to poor performance. As evidence, author Jensen cites his experience at SSRN. They adopted strict adherence to integrity and the organization's productivity rose 300%. FCG has indeed found this link to be accurate in our selection of the Focus Elite firms: strong leadership and healthy cultures lead to greater integrity which leads to greater success.[102]

So, the first good thing about the Erhard and Jensen paper is its practicality: integrity links to performance. To be clear, integrity is not sufficient to ensure long-run value. Successful firms must also "create and execute brilliant competitive, organizational, technological, and human strategies."

Okay, so what is integrity? Beyond just "doing the right thing," how do we carefully define it? Here is the Erhard-Jensen definition:

1. The person's or other human entity's (i.e., firm's) word must be whole, complete, unbroken, sound, in perfect condition.
2. For the word of a person or other human entity (i.e., a firm) to be whole, complete, unbroken, sound, in perfect condition, they must keep their word, or when they will not be keeping their word, they must maintain their word as a whole, complete, etc., by honoring their word.

This definition hinges heavily on clarifying and understanding one's "word." Erhard and Jensen go into great detail about what exactly it means to honor one's word, which is important because they say early on that integrity for a person/firm "is a matter of that person/firm's WORD—nothing more and nothing less." (This heavy emphasis on the "word" is almost biblical: "In the beginning was the Word, and the Word was with God, and the Word was God." Okay, I'll take off my vestments now...) And, here is what they mean by "word" which is the gist of their model: to be in integrity means to live by your word as defined here:

Word-1: What you said you would do or not do

Word-2: What you know to do or not to do

Word-3: What is expected of you by those with whom you desire a workable relationship (that is, their expectations that are in fact unexpressed requests of you), unless you have specifically declined a certain expectation

Word-4: What you say is so (your evidence for what you say is so, would satisfy your listener)

Word-5: What you stand for

Word-6: Moral, ethical, and legal standards of your country and profession

1. The *social* moral standards, the *group* ethical standards, and the *governmental* legal standards of right and wrong, good and bad behavior, in the society, groups, and state in which one enjoys the benefits of membership are also part of one's word (what one is expected to do) unless (a) one has explicitly and publicly expressed an intention not to meet one or more of these standards, and (b) one is willing to bear the costs of refusing to conform to these standards (the rules of the game one is in).

2. For a person or other human entity, **keeping your word** means you fulfill your commitments and promises in full and on time (unlike our "3 out of 10 promises" cited earlier).

3. For a person or other human entity, **honoring your word** means that you either:

- Keep your commitments and promises, and on time, or

- When you have failed (or expect to fail) to keep a commitment or promise on time, you honor your word by:

    - Acknowledging that failure as soon as you realize it, and saying by when you will now keep that word, or that you never will keep that word, and

    - Cleaning up any mess you created for those who were counting on you to keep your word (your commitments and promises) on time.

I'm sure that some of you are ready to stop reading (at best) or pour a drink (at worst) because all this high-faluting jargon is annoying. Understood. (The authors do apologize for the "slogging-through-mud" quality of the writing, but they believe it is necessary for a new understanding of integrity. Think of it as a legal document.) However, the authors are willing—thankfully—to put all this in plain English:

> *Honoring your word means that you are honest and straightforward:*
> *This means nothing is hidden, no deception, no untruths, no violation of*
> *contracts or property rights, etc. Also (as explained earlier), your word*
> *includes conforming to the rules of the games you are in (for example,*
> *ethical standards of the profession or organization you are in, and the*
> *moral standards of the society and legal standards of the government*

entity you are in). If you refuse to play by any of the rules of the games you are in, integrity requires you to make this refusal clear to all others and to willingly bear the costs of doing so. (Gandhi is an example.)"

Much of what Erhard and Jensen are saying is familiar to FCG clients: it's our work on candor and accountability. *Candor* means to speak openly and honestly, not having hidden agendas or "withholds" (i.e., things strategically left unsaid). *Accountability* means making and keeping clear agreements, which includes cleaning up the broken agreements, or "messes" as Erhard and Jensen put it. In this regard, FCG aligns with Erhard's and Jensen's definition of integrity. In addition, we have plenty of evidence to support their view that higher integrity leads to better team performance.

There are, however, some interesting additions and fine points that Erhard and Jensen include in their definitions of keeping one's word.

Word-1. For example, the authors say if someone makes a request of you, then you must do one of four things:
1) accept,
2) decline
3) counter-offer, or
4) promise to respond later at a specific time.

So, they are saying that requests made of me become my word unless I do one of these four things. It is not acting with integrity to duck a request, such as, "Will you come to my meeting this afternoon?" Once the request has landed with you, then integrity requires you to respond. Interestingly, the authors do *not* reverse this concept. If you make a request of someone else, it does *not* become their word to you just because you voiced your request. The authors tie all this rationale back to workability: my efforts to duck requests rather than deal with them cleanly will reduce workability of me and the team. However, for me to assume that my requests of others have now become their word will likely reduce workability. Rather, I should take responsibility for obtaining a response. I like this approach because it is practical—looking at what leads to greater workability—and it rests on the notion of control: what is within my control and what is out of my control? I can control how I respond to people's requests of me. I cannot control how others will respond to my requests of them. Thus, high integrity would look like taking responsibility for those things that are truly in your control.

Word-2. The logic behind this form of "Word" is that we know many things about work, colleagues, clients, processes, etc., and it is not okay to play dumb. For example, a colleague's behavior may signal to you that his actions violate compliance requirements.

For you to have this suspicion and not voice it is a case of "knowing what to do and doing nothing." You can see how the authors' view of integrity highlights these subtle forms of misbehavior: acts of omission.

Word-3. This one is about expectations. This one fascinates me because I routinely ask investment teams and their leaders to get clear about their expectations of each other in order to perform well (i.e., better workability). Teams perform better when expectations are revealed and understood. I ask leaders to write down what they expect of their team, and team members to write down what they expect of their leader. The authors agree that workability will improve as expectations are dealt with. So, teams and leaders should reveal and discuss expectations, with the outcome being agreement on which expectations will become agreements (such as "working from home is acceptable") and which will not. Importantly, to maintain integrity, a person must decline the expectations that she or he has no intention of aligning with. A highly workable team would clear up all these misunderstandings around expectations.

Word-4. This one is about what you allow people to believe. If I create a poorly designed incentive system—one in which staff members are tempted to game it, or one that is simply unfair—then I am out of integrity. As the leader, I may be preaching fairness, teamwork, and transparency, but my compensation and bonus plans don't line up with my words. I allow people to believe that we operate in a meritocracy (where people are rewarded for their contributions), but in truth people are rewarded for longevity, special status (favoritism), mediocre results, and the like. For investment firms that preach meritocracy, a quick test would be to publish everyone's total compensation for the year and see what the staff's reaction would be. In the Focus Elite firms, the reaction would be relatively mild because they tend to practice transparency and few employees are misled in their beliefs about comp. In many other asset management firms, however, the extreme opposite is true: employees would hit the ceiling if they knew what some of their co-workers were making.

Word-5. This one is also fascinating. The notion is that what you stand for is your word. The way you present yourself and behave creates expectations in others about who you are and what you stand for. To the degree that you are misaligned with what you stand for, you are out of integrity. An example of Word-5 in the investment world might be a leader who stands for "client satisfaction," but allows the firm to offer products that clearly are not in the clients' best interests. (Unfortunately, this one happens way too much, in the opinion of FCG.)

Word-6. The authors also consider part of one's word living by the moral, ethical, and legal standards of society and the code of their profession. In the investment world, the code of the profession is best captured in the CFA standards, which all candidates must understand to pass the exam. Of course, one can express an intention *not* to live by certain ones, but then one must accept the consequences, and must let the relevant people know.

To review briefly, the viewpoint of the authors is that integrity is not a moral issue around being a good person vs. being a sneaky rat. It's a question of high performance: high-integrity teams will perform better (higher workability) than low-integrity teams. In the context of FCG's work, this makes sense. Teams that practice high trust, respect, and accountability perform better than "sloppy" teams.

On a practical level, I've already mentioned one exercise that FCG does with leaders and their teams: revealing expectations. Word-3 provides a very useful way to increase workability on a team: *get clarity and agreement around what is expected.* One small cap PM that we work with expected her analysts to bring in one new investment idea each month (12 for the year). In extreme frustration one day, she blurted out, "I just don't understand what is so difficult about coming up with one new idea per month!" I asked her, "Have you made that expectation clear to your team?" Still upset, she responded, "They know that I need new ideas in the portfolio!"

"Yes, but have you specifically told them that you want one new idea per month?" I said. She thought about it for a second and shook her head, "No, not specifically."

At the next investment meeting she made the specific request: one new idea per month. Since that time, the team has responded with new ideas each month. In this way, integrity becomes a very practical matter.

Again, from a practical perspective, look at the Word-4 description about compensation. The authors believe that many of the incentive plans in the investment world are out of integrity. In their words, the plans lead to "unworkability and value destruction. And note that all this destructive behavior by human beings in the firm is motivated by the fact that this common bonus plan is out of integrity in its design as a system. Eliminating this counterproductive behavior [e.g. gaming the system, competing against your teammates] must start by eliminating the lack of integrity in the design of the compensation system. Asking the human beings operating in this badly designed system to change their behavior will fail unless and until the compensation system itself is redesigned to put it into integrity."

Some time ago, FCG came to the same conclusion: many incentive plans for asset managers are poorly designed. As a result, FCG began doing compensation (FCG calls it "reward design") work for firms. Our approach is radically different from that of the big-name compensation firms in the industry. Instead of using a lot of shared industry data to show investment leaders how they should compensate their staff, we start with a radically simple premise: intelligent professionals can design their own compensation plans. (One leader responded in horror to this idea: "You are turning the keys over to the inmates!" You do have to wonder about his leadership style when he uses this metaphor …) In our experience of collaborating with the very professionals who are being rewarded, we have never seen the process fail. It usually requires two meetings, of two to three hours each, to get the plan mostly done—and the integrity is intact because the team has thoroughly discussed the options and come to their own agreement about what constitutes a fair, transparent, competitive, and understandable (i.e., simple-enough) plan. If the planning session starts to head in the direction of "out of integrity," then invariably the team will self-police itself back into integrity. This approach works well. The real beauty of it is that you achieve a high level of buy-in when the team signs off on a collaboratively designed plan. No one complains at the end of the year when bonuses are paid.

Personally, since reading Erhard's and Jensen's paper, I can sense a renewed interest in living in integrity. The clarity of their definition of *integrity*—living by one's word—has inspired me to be as transparent and clear as I can be with friends, family, colleagues, and clients. The reward is a very "clean" sense of personal integrity, which results in higher energy levels and a very clear conscience. Things like hidden agendas and half-truths weigh us down and cause lower performance levels.

Isn't it interesting that an industry in which "integrity" is the number-one value chosen on culture surveys has achieved the lowest trust rating on the Edelman Trust Barometer?[103] Clearly, we have work to do. And you contributed to the improvement by reading this article. Now, be careful with those New Year's resolutions …

---

101 Werner Erhard and Michael Jensen, "Putting Integrity into Finance: A Purely Positive Approach" (April 5, 2012; revised November 5, 2015), http://papers.ssrn.com/sol3/papers.cfm?abstract_id=1985594 All quotes are from this paper.

102 See FCG, "Linking Strong Culture to Investment Success" (2014), http://www.focuscgroup.com/wp-content/uploads/2015/11/Linking_Strong_Culture_to_Success.pdf

103 See the latest results at https://www.edelman.com/trust-barometer. The reference to "lowest" was after the 2008 crash.

Appendix B: Managing Millennials: They Are Different

Should you worry about "generational differences"? That's today's question. After all, people are people, so shouldn't you treat them all the same? With respect and dignity. Fairness. Trust. Same old stuff. Right?

Well, yes.

But according to the top dog at Gallup, when asked, "Are millennials really that different?" Jim Clifton responded, "Profoundly so." FCG agrees, having seen their impact on investment cultures. Of course, not all investment leaders see it that way. Table B.1 is a vote from a roomful of investment leaders on the topic of managing millennials.

Table B.1 Managing Millennials

Managing Millennials effectively is an important topic	
Agree	90%
Neutral	0%
Disagree	10%

Two dissenting votes: And these two leaders were not dragging their knuckles and breathing heavily through their mouths—quite the opposite. They were sharp, good leaders. Their rationale on voting no: "If you are a good manager, then you need to understand your people and deal with each of them individually." Each *did* manage millennials and was doing it successfully because they *were* acknowledging the uniqueness of each employee. What these two excellent leaders failed to realize is that many of us could use a "heads up" regarding millennials, those born between 1981 and 1996. We don't necessarily see them as different, so we make the mistake—in our busy work days—of treating them like boomers, born between 1946 and 1964. Even if we do see the millennial difference, it still doesn't answer the question: So, what are the new rules, according to millennials? And how does a firm respond to them?" FCG's experience with millennials reveals five major changes to be aware of:

1. Purpose
2. Development (which includes lots of feedback)
3. Autonomy (made possible by technology)
4. Transparency
5. Social causes

Purpose

Gallup describes it as "purpose over paycheck." A survey of millennials showed the following shocker: More than 60% would rather make $40K in a job they love than $100K in one they think is boring. One of the participants in the roomful mentioned earlier commented, "I tried to influence my millennial daughter to go into investing and she stopped me and said, 'Mom, I'd rather drown myself. I like working in a rescue shelter.'" Okay, then. Boomers and Xers (the "older generations") seem to understand the millenials' drive for purpose, as they chose it above all other motivational factors in the vote shown in Table B.2.

Table B.2 Motivational Factors

Top 3 factors in Millennial engagement	
Purpose	23%
Development Opportunities	20%
Recognition	17%
Feedback	15%
Peers	10%
Boss	7%
Autonomy	4%
Compensation	4%

If you want to engage millennials, you need to understand their desire to do something meaningful—and understand that *meaningful* does NOT mean "make a lot of money." Investment leaders must be able to articulate why their firm is contributing to a better society. In FCG's view, this should be an easy task, but many older leaders have trouble with it. They've never really thought about it. They are practical people who are deep into running the firm. Purpose doesn't really enter their thinking. So, as a leader of millennials, be able to articulate a solid reason why (and how) the firm contributes to a better world. For example: "Our firm exists to positively influence people's financial lives."[104] See? It doesn't have to be tricky, just clear and purposeful. And sincere.

Development

Note that in Table B.2, the second highest vote-getter is "development opportunities." FCG sees this factor in all of the culture work we do. The biggest gap value in firms—that is, the difference between what firms "have" and what they "want"—is "leadership development/mentoring." To show you how millennial-dependent this factor is, look at the "want" vote in one firm when we slice the data by age groups. Employees at the same firm were asked to select 10 values that they want more of. Table B.3 is what the boomers said.

Table B.3 Top-Ten Values–Aspirational Culture: Baby Boomer

	# of Responses	ABC Firm Percent
Client satisfaction	26	59%
Ethical/Integrity	25	57%
Collaboration/Teamwork	25	57%
Excellence/Continuous mprovement	24	55%
Results oriented	20	45%
Professional	17	39%
Respect	17	39%
Meritocracy	17	39%
Balance (home/work)	16	36%
Accountability/Responsibility long-term perspective/vision, loyalty tied)	12	27%

N = 44

Notice, there is no demand for "leadership development/mentoring." Now look what the same firm's millennials said, in Table B.4.

Table B.4 Top-Ten Values–Aspirational Culture: Generation Y

	# of Responses	ABC Firm Percent
Collaboration/Teamwork	63	47%
Excellence/Continuous improvement	61	46%
Ethical/Integrity	55	41%
Leadership development/Mentoring	51	38%
Balance (home/work)	49	37%
Meritocracy	47	35%
Client satisfaction	46	35%
Professional	44	33%
Respect	37	28%
Creativity/Innovation	37	28%

N = 133

Notice that "leadership development/mentoring" comes out as the fourth highest aspirational value, with nearly 40% of the millennials choosing it.

This is a typical response at investment firms. So, what are the millennials asking for? They want career paths: *What's next for me? How do I learn new skills and progress?* They want coaching and mentoring: *Who will show me the ropes and take a sincere interest in my development?* They want feedback, and lots of it. In other words, they want attention. They had it from their "helicopter" parents and from their teachers, now they want it at work. When millennials quit, the exit interviews often reveal, *"I wasn't getting enough face time with my boss."* So, if you want to keep your talented millennials, you'd better find a way to meet these needs.

Autonomy

Millennials have grown up with technology, so they understand that knowledge work can be done anywhere. Their mantra is, "work is something you do, not a place you go."[105] Old-school bosses have to reprogram their minds to understand this. FCG has responded to this new reality by partnering with Jody Thompson, co-author of the book *Why Work Sucks and How to Fix it*. Jody developed the Results-Only-Work-Environment (ROWE) concept and has implemented it globally for firms. She has helped boomers understand the shift from face time to results-only. We introduced Jody to two investment firms, each one a top firm as measured by leadership, culture, and performance. Interestingly, one firm embraced ROWE and in short order moved to practices like no vacation policy and no office hours. (In other words, take vacation when you want and spend as much or as little time at the office as you wish. Just make sure you deliver results. Jody is fond of saying, "No results, No job.") The second firm could not make the mental shift and balked at the program. The first firm's CEO told us recently that productivity, in his view, has increased. The second firm still struggles with bouts of employee discontent, as workers complain about being treated unfairly in the "flex-time" arrangement. With ROWE there is complete autonomy, so all the grumbling about fair flex time goes away! Here's the catch: Managers in ROWE need to be very clear about roles, responsibilities, and deliverables—in other words: *accountability*.

Transparency

Millennials expect full transparency in the workplace. They are suspicious of "need-to-know" communication policies. Old-school, command-and-control thinking revolves around the concept that leaders have the information/solutions and workers execute their orders. This approach was fully prevalent in the 1950s and 1960s. (and made sense given the difference between factory worker roles and knowledge worker roles.) As the workplace shifts from command-and-control to facilitative leadership, where collaboration is the rule, the millennials are asking the obvious question: "Why can't we have full access to information?" The knee-jerk response from many boomer bosses is a chest-grab of fear: "Are you kidding?! We'd lose all control!" To be clear, some information requires confidentiality for legal reasons or for reasons of integrity (e.g., a promise made to *not* share information). We understand that. Far too often, though, leaders withhold information because "we've never shared it before." In other words, there is no valid reason to withhold; it's just the way it has always been done. FCG has seen many cases of increased trust, respect, and morale when leaders open the kimono and begin to share more and more information with staff members.

Causes

Millennials' interest in causes extends well beyond pledging to United Way. Millennials have logged more volunteer hours in their short lives than the Xers and boomers have combined. Investment firms that allow themselves to be a conduit for volunteer opportunities will attract millennials. Increasingly, FCG's clients have set up foundations to support worthwhile causes. A client example: *The mission of our Foundation is to make a positive impact by actively engaging all employees in identifying and supporting charitable organizations of excellence.* Another client donates 50% of profits to its foundation which actively engages in causes like ending genocide on the planet. Talk to your employees. Find out what they care about. Get involved.

Solutions and Common Ground

Wise leaders will pay attention to the needs of millennials because they will constitute more than half of the workforce by 2020. FCG offers these tips:

1. Accept that millennials bring new values and attitudes to the workplace and respond accordingly. The "Big 5" discussed earlier in this appendix are important to millennials and must be addressed in some measure. If you wish to attract and retain top young talent, then you must build a desirable workplace. Millennials differ from prior generations in that they are quick to assess and leave poor cultures. (Boomers leave jobs after 7 years, Xers after 5, and millennials after 2.)

2. Recognize and leverage the common ground areas:

   • **Collaboration/teamwork.** As you saw in the preceding culture survey results (ABC firm), all generations embrace collaboration. So, you can always bring conflict back to, "We all want to work well as a team." Invoke mutual purpose and work out a solution.

   • **Respect/trust.** These pillars of strong culture are also important to both generations. Willingness to understand and respect different viewpoints builds trust. Take a curious stance toward different values. Don't be the leader in the Figure B.5 cartoon.

Figure B.5 Don't be this guy...

Courtesy of WuMo by Mikael Wulff and Anders Morganthaler

   • **Accountability.** Each generation accuses the other of being "entitled." Entitlement ends when accountability starts. FCG has found that all generations embrace accountability. The key is to create accountability while eliminating fear and blame. This can be done through clear roles, responsibilities, decision rights, and goals. Plus, skillful feedback: both positive and negative. FCG has yet to hear talented millennials or boomers say, *"No way. We do NOT want that sort of accountability here!"*

Returning to our two dissenting leaders mentioned earlier, we applaud them for doing a fine job managing millennials. Our advice to them? Keep up the good work, but please, don't tout the idea that *"all generations are the same, just be a good manager and you'll do fine."* Why? Many of us are not born leaders and we need all the help we can get. The tips offered in this appendix will help. If you ignore them, you may lose some talented workers—and it won't be like the old days where they "quit and stay." They will quit and leave!

---

[104] Thanks to Michael Falk on our team, as he first suggested this purpose statement which was the driving force behind his recently published book on entitlements and sustainable economic growth. See his website for more on *Let's All Learn How to Fish*: www.letsalllearnhowtofish.com

[105] A quote from Jody Thompson, originator of the concept of a "Results-Only Work Environment." For more on results-only work environments, see Jody's website: www.gorowe.com.

Appendix C: Strategy: Can You Say What Yours Is?

An article in The *Economist* was entitled, "Fund Management will invest for food."[106] I recommend this piece for your non-investment staff, as it nicely summarizes the challenges that all investment firms are facing ... and why salaries and/or headcount may be shrinking. In a rather chilling statement, the article proclaims, "Like shoppers on a budget, investors are trading down from expensive brands to white-label goods. That may put many active managers out of a job." Warren Buffett himself, the hero of active management, is quoted in the piece: "My advice to the trustee [of my personal portfolio] could not be more simple: put 10% of the cash in short-term government bonds and 90% in a very low-cost S&P 500 index fund." Ouch. From our own hero, this damning statement! The body of the article goes into detail about fee pressure, smart beta alternatives, and shrinking DB markets. Indeed, the writer expresses surprise that "commoditization of the fund-management industry has not happened sooner. After all, the first low-cost tracking fund, designed to mimic the performance of the S&P 500 index, was created more than 40 years ago. The slow transition is partly a result of how most funds are bought and sold: the commissions for brokers that made it attractive to push managed funds, and the fact that many people buy their investment products through banks."

All is not lost. Active managers will *not* disappear overnight. Hedge funds and private equity managers are cited as alternatives to traditional long-only investing, and three types of investors—the three largest—are still interested in the active managers: (1) sovereign wealth, (2) DB funds, and (3) high-net-worth individuals.

After throwing this bone to investment managers, the writer concludes, "Life will be harder for traditional active-fund management companies … Investors of the world, unite! You have nothing to lose but your fund managers' fees." (Shhhhh … not so loud!)

Which leads directly to the meat of this appendix. Given the environment described in the *Economist* article, can you say what your strategy is? (We use this language on purpose because a very fine article from the *Harvard Business Review* carried this title.[107]) FCG has been doing strategy retreats with investment firms for many years. Our experience is that few firms do strategy well. Rich Horwath, best-selling author of books on strategy, agrees with this view: "A survey of more than 2,000 global executives found that only 19 percent of managers said that their companies have a distinct process for developing strategy. For those firms that do have a process for strategy development, an alarming 67 percent of managers said that their organization is bad at developing strategy … . Most managers know that [strategy] is important, but few do it effectively." Inquiring into why this is the case, Horwath identified the top reasons for poor strategy (Table C.1).

Table C.1 Reasons for Poor Strategy

Strategy challenge	% of organization citing each
Time	96%
Commitment (buy-in)	72%
Lack of priorities	60%
Status quo	56%
Not understanding what strategy is	48%

FCG's experience supports Horwath's findings. Many firms label their year-end budget planning as strategy. It is not. McKinsey reports that "[a] fresh strategic insight—something your company sees that no one else does—is one of the foundations of competitive advantage. It helps companies focus their resources on moves that separate them from the pack. Only 35 percent of 2,135 global executives believed their strategies rested on unique and powerful insights." Horwath developed his own assessment for strategy and has used it with more than 500 companies. He writes, "The average score is 45 percent, a failing grade, indicating there are many rudderless companies out there that are strategically adrift." Okay, maybe Horwath is just trying to sell his books and services, but in truth we see his findings borne out in many investment firms. They are often great money managers (despite what The *Economist* says) and very bright thinkers, but not strategic. Authors Birshan and Kan, in an article about strategy, write, "We are entering the age of the strategist. Rare is the company, though, where all members of the top team have well-developed strategic muscles."[108] (FCG did a leadership offsite with a hedge fund where the skill in shortest supply—by the firm's own self-assessment—was "strategic thinking.") Two separate studies on leaders and the most sought-after skills cited strategic thinking as number one.

To help leaders develop their strategy skills, Horwath wrote a primer on strategy called *Deep Dive*.[109] FCG uses it as our foundational book on doing strategy work. (Horwath has also written a sequel, *Elevate*.[110]) Probably the most useful tool for leadership teams aspiring to do excellent strategy work is a common language. In this regard Horwath is good. He introduces nice distinctions and clarity which allow for productive strategy discussions. (FCG has seen strategy sessions devolve into time-sucking arguments over what words mean: *milestone, tactic, objective, goal, outcome, mission,* etc.) We adapted Horwath's GOST formula, which is simple and powerful (see Table C.2).

Table C.2 Adapted GOST Formula

GOAL	OBJECTIVE	STRATEGY	TACTIC
What	What	How	How
General	Specific	General	Specific

GOAL = General statement of desired outcome: "Weight loss"

OBJECTIVE = Spefic statement of desired outcome: "10 pounds"

STRATEGY = General statement of HOW the goal will be achieved: "more excercise, healthier food choices

TACTICS = Specific statements of HOW the goal will be achieved: "join the healthclub, eliminate sugar and wheat from diet"

As simple as these definitions are, they do streamline strategy discussions. So, to sum up so far:

1) Most investment firms do *not* allocate sufficient time to strategy work. (They mistake year-end budget planning for actual strategy.)
2) Most investment firms have not developed a framework—including clear language—for doing good strategy work. (They are overconfident about their ability to develop excellent strategies.)

3) The investment environment is increasingly demanding that firms actually have strategic business plans. ("[Commoditization] may put many active managers out of a job.")

So, what's to be done? Horwath suggests five key questions to ask when considering whether to change or reassess your firm's strategy. For the investment firm, they look like this:

1) **Have our firm's goals been achieved or changed?** (*Goals* are what you're trying to achieve; *strategy* is how you're going to get there.) If you have capped two investment funds because they've reached optimal size, then it's time to think about next steps. Or, if your client base is disappearing—current situation for many traditional bond managers—you may need to change your goals.

2) **Have the clients' needs changed?** Clearly this is the challenge for many active managers. As *The Economist* article pointed out, clients are getting more sophisticated and driving harder deals. Clients now refer to the "fund of funds" model as the "fees on fees" business. To win in this space now, your value proposition has to be much more sharply defined and clear to clients. And it must actually add value.

3) **Is there new value in the marketplace?** Truly innovative thinkers are reacting to the new environment with novel products. For example, Research Affiliates introduced their smart beta product—the Fundamental Index—years ago, and it has rapidly grown into a powerhouse.

4) **Have competitors changed the perception of value in the market?** Again, the idea used to be that beta was the default choice of passive investing. Now firms are producing their own smart beta strategies as alternatives to high-cost active management.

5) **What is the condition of your capabilities?** Have you honestly, humbly assessed your firm's capabilities (i.e., the products/services you offer)? Relative to your competitors, have your capabilities strengthened or weakened? If they are stronger, leverage them. If they have lost ground, it may be time to revisit them and make them fully competitive or exit the market.

So, meet with the senior team and give these questions some serious consideration.[111] Also, we recommend both of Horwath's books and the article mentioned above: Can You Say What Your Strategy Is? (Amusing strategy trivia: Did you know that strategy guru Michael Porter—author of *Competitive Strategy*[112]—ran a strategy consulting firm that went bankrupt? It's true. "Those who can, do ...")

Most importantly, challenge yourself that you are not simply in denial about strategy. It's easy to cling to the status quo and rationalize that everything will return to normal.

Do you believe that? Do you *really* believe that? if not, assemble your best strategic thinkers and get busy designing a path for the new reality. A good place to start? These basic questions:

1. **Why** do we exist? What is our mission?
2. **Where** are we heading? What is our vision of success?
3. **How** will we get there? What is our strategy?
4. **What** is happening in our firm and the industry? What does a SWOT analysis look like for our firm?
5. **Who** are we as a firm? What is our firm's culture? Is it the right culture to achieve our mission?

Try this exercise. Write your answers to these questions on paper. Read them to your colleagues. Get the dialogue started.

---

106 "Fund Management: Will Invest for Food," *The Economist* (May 1, 2014), http://www.economist.com/news/briefing/21601500-books-and-music-investment-industry-being-squeezed-will-invest-food

107 David Collis and Michael G. Rukstad, "Can You Say What Your Strategy Is?" Harvard Business Review (April, 2008).

108 Birshan and Kan, "Becoming more strategic: Three tips for any executive," *McKinsey Quarterly* (July 2012).

109 Rich Horwath, *Deep Dive* (Greenleaf Book Group, 2009), https://www.amazon.com/Deep-Dive-Rich-Horwath-author/dp/B0092I0ALK/ref=pd_lpo_sbs_14_img_1?_encoding=UTF8&psc=1&refRID=8DRXK9VNVFKXR7018QVK

110 Rich Horwath, *Elevate: The Three Disciplines of Advanced Strategic Thinking* (Wiley, 2014).

111 Additionally, you might ask FCG's Michael Falk to join the conversation. Michael is our expert in combining strategy methods with deep investment expertise. With his background as a chief investment officer and as a strategy consultant with FCG, he is uniquely qualified to think through your current strategy and decide what, if anything, should be done. Contact Michael at mfalk@focusCgroup.com

112 Michael Porter, *Competitive Strategy* (Free Press, 1998).

Appendix D: Strategy: Sales–It's a Brave New World

Selling has changed dramatically in the investment world. I remember well the "old" version: a likeable person, with an easy smile, a credit card, access to tickets, and a decent golf game. In my second week as an analyst (1980), I met a salesman who asked me nonchalantly if I followed Chicago sports. Naively, I responded, "Yes, I'm a long-suffering Bears fan." I thought he was just making conversation. Next week there were two 50-yard-line tickets to Sunday's game on my desk. (In those days it was okay to accept such gifts … .)

Now salespeople have become investment experts, with MBAs and CFAs. Some have prior experience managing money. In addition to this subject matter expertise, today's top salespeople have carefully honed skills for consultative selling. Two books are essential reads, in my view. The first is *Let's Get Real or Let's Not Play*[113] by Khalsa and

Illig. This book offers invaluable advice on how to plan for, execute, and follow up prospect/client meetings. I reread it every year-end. The second book, which I'll describe in this essay, is called *The Challenger Sale*.[114] Many are familiar with this book, as it has essentially gone viral.

To summarize the challenger approach: Traditional selling is relationship based, aiming to build a trusting and comfortable relationship with the buyer/client, whereas challenger selling aims at going beyond the comfort goal and creating a healthy tension with buyers/clients by providing them new insights about their business. Another way to think of challenger selling is that instead of asking "what keeps you up at night?" the salesperson goes in with a well-reasoned hypothesis about the industry and common problems, then provides insights and solutions that are tailored to the particular buyer/client. The goal of the challenger discussion is to get a client reaction of: "Gee, that's interesting. I hadn't thought of that." One way to put this is that challenger sellers are more interested in being memorable than in being agreeable.

The road map for achieving this outcome is shown in Table D.1.

Table D.1 Challenger Selling–Commercial Teaching Pitch

Stage	Commentary
1 Warmer	Align and build rapport around client challenges they are facing. Lead with "hypothesis": your view of what problem and solution could be.
2 Reframe	Reframe and show unrecognized problem, based on collaborattion with marketing (not a flash of new insight in the moment). Define the client needs rather than respond to them.
3 Rational drowning	Intensify the problem.
4 Emotional impact	Humanize the problem, make real.
5 Value propisition–a new way	A new solution, tied to your firm's core.
6 Your solution	A path to implementation: don't leave "alone in the desert".

The success of this approach depends on several of your firm's tribes working closely together. So, if your firm is troubled by tribal warfare, you'll have more difficulty implementing this approach. Specifically, marketing, sales, and investments all must collaborate to develop insights that form a "hypothesis." For example, after reading Casey Quirk's piece, "Life after Benchmarks,"[115] your firm could brainstorm what products and solutions you offer that go beyond the traditional benchmarks and actually address client needs.

To give readers a feel for how this approach could work, I will use FCG as an example.

1. **Warmer:** In the "warmer phase" we ask: What is a common problem that all investment firms face? For us, the answer is talent. Investment firms depend on strong talent to win in the markets. Losing good talent is a major problem for firms. The best firms are able to attract and retain good people. Many firms that lose talent are blindsided; they don't see it coming. Or, they see signs of a problem but they wait too long to deal with it. They only react when they are in crisis.

2. **Reframe:** Investment firms will all agree that talent is crucial to success, so nothing new has been introduced at this point. The reframe is: Early diagnosis is the key to talent retention. As in medicine, finding problems early makes all the difference. That is why people have annual check-ups. The reframe for investment firms is: Don't be reactive (waiting until there is a crisis); rather, be proactive (catching any issues early and dealing with them). Get an annual check-up.

3. **Rational Drowning:** This step involves facts and data. FCG can present numerous cases of firms that ignored their talent issues and suffered huge setbacks as a result. My personal favorite example is a hedge fund, in which the CEO of the parent company asked the two leaders of the hedge fund to meet with FCG to learn more about our services. The CEO had a hunch that the leaders of the hedge fund might be dealing with some personal issues that were going untreated. During the FCG presentation, the two hedge fund leaders busily worked their smartphones and rarely looked up at us. Eventually, I said, "Of course, some people don't think leadership and culture is important to investment firm success." Both hedge fund leaders, still looking down at their devices, put their hands in the air, signifying, "That would be us!" The CEO and I smiled at one another and realized that the pitch was going nowhere. The outcome? Within a year, the hedge fund collapsed because the two leaders got into a power struggle that couldn't be resolved. FCG has countless stories like this. Overload the prospect with stories that illustrate the dire consequences of ignoring the problem.

4. **Emotional Impact:** The goal of step 4 is to take the buyer/client from "Interesting, but that doesn't really apply to us" to "Wow, that could happen to us." The stories that are useful here are the ones that FCG has seen with clients that were completely blindsided by the loss of key talent—and there are many. We well remember congratulating a CEO about the recent successes that his firm had enjoyed, only to

learn that a week later his crown-jewel investment team was lifted out by another firm. In another case, the CEO was aware that his lead PM was unhappy about current circumstances, but assumed that the trouble would blow over. Within a few weeks, the lead PM was lifted out with nearly all the team. The two firms in question are still battling it out in the courts. Another situation involved a younger team of small-cap managers who believed they should be given more freedom to run their product in their own way. About eight months after the trouble started, FCG was called in to help patch up the situation. By then, the younger investment professionals were beyond redemption: They wanted out. The situation had gotten too toxic in their view and they wanted a fresh start. In all of these cases, there was a point in time when the teams were performing well and the firm leaders assumed that it would continue indefinitely. In fact, the trouble was already brewing, yet the CEOs were still blindsided.

5. **A New Way:** Here is where the seller introduces a solution. In this case, not FCG's specific solution, but a general solution. In medical terms, the seller gives the case for early diagnosis and treatment. Firms that conscientiously review their talent and comp each year and check in with key personnel are far better off than the ones that assume everything is fine. The best practice that offers a solution is to be proactive around talent. Typically, if a problem is brewing, a third party will be better able to discover it than the leaders who have created it.

6. **Your Solution:** this is the final step in which you show the buyer/client that your solution is better able to address the problem than anything or anyone else. Notice that you wait until step 6 to trot out your company's offering. FCG has several proven diagnostics that allow for early detection of problems with a firm's talent. Through surveys and interviews, FCG can deliver a "health report" on the various teams and key opinion leaders in the firm. If the health report is fine, great! If not, you have a much better chance of treating the problem appropriately because you've discovered it early.

The authors of the *Challenger Sale* summarize this six-step process as follows: you've taught the client something new and valuable about its business (which is what they were looking for from the conversation), in a way that specifically leads them to value your capabilities over those of the competition (which is what you were looking for from the conversation).

I find this approach intriguing. In FCG's case, we can offer many different hypotheses, not just this one about losing key talent. For example, what about Red Xs? (Red Xs are the brilliant but difficult stars who populate the investment industry. See Chapter 6 on Red Xs.) Early diagnosis of Red Xs can also be invaluable. Many firms hang on to Red

Xs because they do deliver incredible value. But at what cost? We know a PM who has created a brilliant track record in long-only equity portfolios but has turned over the analyst staff 200% in four years and even more in a few targeted sectors! No one wants to work with him. The environment is so toxic under his leadership that many analysts leave without having lined up new jobs. Early diagnosis in this case would allow for the installation of a co-PM (they have such a talented person on staff), which would then allow senior management to tell the toxic PM "shape up or we'll ship you out." In another instance, a toxic Red X was the CIO. He was deemed too valuable to fire because the firm would lose many clients. Well, they ended up losing clients anyway because the two most talented PMs left, went across the street, started their own firm, and took the half the clients with them. All because the CIO was a jerk. In both cases, early detection and treatment would have greatly benefited the firms in question.

So, now that you get the idea of this, how does it work for your firm? What is a hypothesis you could put forward to challenge your buyers/clients? If you are a single-product, long-only, active equity manager, what could you say to clients? Here's one thought. Assuming that you have identified the edge you have in the markets—and hopefully you have, or else that is your first piece of business!—then you could state that as an industry condition all buyers/clients are facing the same problem: finding consistent alpha producers. After you've "warmed up" the buyer/client with an awareness that alpha is hard to find on a consistent basis, you then provide a reframe: No firm will find alpha if it is battling short-termism. If the asset manager is publicly traded or owned by a parent company that insists on quarterly results, then—you could argue—it is doomed to mediocrity (or worse). Your firm's pitch might be: We are independent, so we can truly take a long-term perspective. This long-term orientation allows us to produce alpha consistently over a cycle. This is the pitch that one of our successful clients uses, with good results.

Alternatively, consider a multiproduct firm that can offer more sophisticated solutions. Such a firm can warm up the buyer/client with a statement about the new demand for complete solutions rather than single products. The reframe can be: In the past, providers aimed at beating benchmarks, whereas we embrace the new approach that YOU are the benchmark. So, we'll design a customized approach based on your specific needs (think goals—future liabilities-based) and create your solution with our products, or at least those that fit. Again, we know a client who is offering this reframe and using the challenger approach with good success.

As one who loves thought leadership, I find this whole challenger approach fascinating. What is your hypothesis? What is your reframe? What is the unique insight that you are offering? Regardless of whether you adopt the whole challenger sales approach, you can certainly play with these questions. A Greenwich survey indicates that 56% of the drivers of relationship quality are service, *not* investments.[116] Our experience supports this finding: the New Era in investments is about both client service and investment performance. Finding new and better ways to interact with clients is crucial to success going forward.

---

[113] Mahan Khalsa and Randy Illig, *Let's Get Real or Let's Not Play* (Portfolio, 2008), https://www.amazoncom/s/?ie=UTF8&keywords=let%27s+get+real+or+let%27s+not+play&tag= googhydr-20&index=aps&hvadid=241664017607&hvpos=1t1&hvnetw=g&hvrand= 1296566173741324569&hvpone=&hvptwo=&hvqmt=e&hvdev=c&hvdvcmdl=&hvlocint= &hvlocphy=9021457&hvtargid=kwd-1125864422&ref=pd_sl_32y9rew06f_e

[114] Matthew Dixon and Brent Adamson, *The Challenger Sale* (Penguin, 2011), https://www.amazon. com/Challenger-Sale-Control-Customer-Conversation/dp/1591844355/ref=sr_1_2?ie=UTF8&qid= 1525900537&sr=8-2&keywords=let%27s+get+real+or+let%27s+not+play

[115] Casey Quirk, "Life after Benchmarks" (November 2013), http://www.caseyquirk.com/whitepapers.html

[116] [Greenwich survey]

Appendix E: Feedback–Learning to Love It

Feedback is at the heart of high-performing investment teams. The best firms we know excel at creating cultures of feedback. But it's hard. One friend adamantly believes that no one wants negative feedback! Let's explore that belief and see what can be done to unwind it. The best resource I know of on feedback is *Thanks for the Feedback*[117] by Stone and Heen. It's long but entertaining and rich with wisdom.

First, why are we resistant to feedback, even when we *know* that we should be open to it? Stone and Heen do a nice job of summarizing the three main reasons why we push away feedback (Table E.1).

Table E.1 Reasons for Avoiding Feedback

Triggers (reasons for getting defensive)	Description
Truth triggers ("that's just wrong")	When we hear feedback that seems just plain wrong, we tend to dismiss it. We become offended and push back. Example (John to Sally): "Sally, I heard some feedback that people think of you as aloof and arrogant." Sally: "Aloof and arrogant? That's ridiculous. I may be a lot of things, but I am not aloof and arrogant!" (Uh-oh, sounds kind of aloof and arrogant!)
Relationship triggers ("consider the source")	When we receive feedback from someone who may have a "hidden agenda," we dismiss it because of the source. We shift our focus from the feedback itself to the person delivering it ("You cannot trust anything he says"). Separately, we dismiss people who don't have the proper credentials ("He doesn't have a CFA, so I wouldn't pay much attention").
Identity triggers (threaten our security, approval, or control)	When we feel that feedback threatens our needs for security, approval, or control, we often become defensive. We tend to reject feedback when we are "below the line"—and the big factors for going below are a fear of losing security, approval, and control. Example: "Poor work like this will cost you your job." Forget about the person absorbing any feedback after hearing those words!

Useful distinctions like the sample triggers in Table E.1 are why the *Feedback* book is so good. The authors have thought a lot about feedback and have built helpful models. In addition to pointing out problems—like becoming defensive—the authors have great ideas for solutions. Consider these helpful tips for the three triggers described in Table E.1 (Table E.2).

Table E.2 Shifting Trigger Responses

Triggered Reaction	Learning Responses (vs. defensive response)
Truth trigger: That's just wrong That's not accurate That's crazy	Shift from "that's wrong" to "Tell me more…" or "Help me understand…" Before you reject the feedback, try it on like a new suit of clothes. Ask yourself, "How could this be true about me?" Use the 2% rule: surely there must be at least 2% useful information in their feedback.
Relationship trigger: After all I've done for you? Who are you to say? You're the problem, not me.	Don't switchtrack: Separate the feedback from the person delivering it. Say, "It's true, you have done a lot of good for me, but let's stick with the feedback right now…" Step back to see the relationship system between giver and receiver, and the ways you are each contributing to the problems that are prompting you to exchange feedback, and just consider the feedback. Is it useful? Again, the 2% rule.
Identity trigger: I screw up everything. I'm doomed. That feedback threatens my (security, approval, control).	Learn how your mental and emotional "wiring" affects the way you hear and react to feedback. Dismantle distortions: see feedback at "actual size." (It's easy to jump to "all or none" thinking.) Cultivate a growth identity (vs. a fixed mindset). Make a commitment to learning instead of being right.

Another useful tool that the authors introduce is sorting feedback into one of three buckets. Any feedback we receive as professionals can usually be categorized as shown in Table E.3.

Table E.3 Feedback Buckets

Type of Feedback	Giver's Purpose
Appreciation	To see, acknowledge, connect, motivate, thank
Coaching	To help the receiver expand knowledge, sharpen skill, improve capability
Evaluation	To rate or rank against a set of standards, to align expectations, to inform decision making

First off, the three types of feedback make a nice acronym: ACE (which so far has allowed me to remember it!). Second, in my experience these three types of feedback are very useful. However, they are also very different. The authors do a nice job of giving examples of "misfires," where a person wants appreciation but instead gets coaching. Or she wants an evaluation and instead gets appreciation. So, a good first question in response to a request for feedback could be: What kind do you want? Appreciation, coaching, or evaluation?

The authors remind us of many important feedback basics along the way. These include the ideas that good feedback is:

1. Timely (as close to the event as possible, such as right after the presentation)
2. Specific ("your hand gestures were very effective" and not simply "great speech")
3. Genuine (honestly felt, not forced flattery)

The thing that separates this book from the myriad of other manuals on feedback is the authors' practical advice on tricky situations. The book is long because the authors take the time to parse difficult examples from work (and personal) life. For example, most feedback is delivered in shorthand or "labels," such as "be a team player" or "be more proactive." The giver and receiver assume that the communication is clear (i.e., they both understand what is being said). But these bumper stickers get us into trouble because in fact we do not have the same understanding as the other person. Again, the authors provide good examples of miscommunication, as in the sample in Table E.4.

Table E.4 Feedback Miscommunication

Coaching Feedback	What was heard	What was meant
Be more confident	Give people the impression that you know things even if you don't.	Have the confidence to say you don't know when you don't know.

Evaluation Feedback	What was heard	What was meant
You've received a rating of 4 out of 5 this year.	Last year I got a 4. I worked so much harder this year and got another 4. Hard work isn't noticed.	No one gets a 5. Few get a 4 and now you've done it twice! You are doing outstanding work.

The message here is: *Spot the labels*. When giving or receiving feedback, spot the labels and dig underneath them for what they actually mean.

In the course of providing great tips on feedback, the authors align closely with what FCG has been teaching and practicing for years, concepts like "fact" and "story." (Of course, we like this!) The model they offer is shown in Figure E.1.

Figure E.1 "Coming-From" and "Going-To" Model

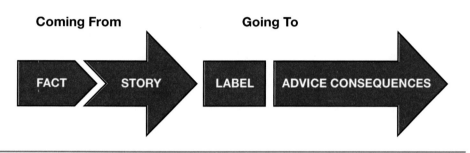

In using this model, be clear about (1) where the feedback is coming from and (2) which parts are fact and which parts are story (interpretation). What label has been placed on the feedback? (E.g., "You are not a team player.") Then look at what the advice or consequence is.

The authors double-click on the final arrow in Figure E.1—advice and consequences— and offer these useful questions for when you are receiving feedback.

When receiving coaching feedback, ask these questions:

Looking back	LABEL	Looking forward
What did you observe about me, about the world, about whatever matters to this topic? What can you see that I can't? (blindspot)	Label that captures the feedback in general (e.g., "More proactive")	What's your advice? What would I do or say to implement that advice? Show me, model it, give me an example.

When receiving evaluation feedback, ask these questions:

Looking back	LABEL	Looking forward
What were the criteria you used? What did you consider to be most important? Are there concerns I should know about? Are there skills or experience that I am missing?	Label that captures the feedback in general (e.g., "Not a team player")	What are the consequences? How will this affect me in the coming year? What should I be thinking about or working on? When might we reassess?

An important skill in feedback is what the authors call "right spotting." It is easy to identify and point out all the wrong things; we are wonderful critics. But can you balance that ability with spotting what is right? Specifically, they recommend the exercise of spotting what's different in your points of view about the feedback, and then identifying what is correct or "right" about the feedback. An example is given in Table E.5.

Table E.5 Feedback Example

Feedback	What's Different?	What's Right?
Margie learns that she doesn't get the promotion to be the new department head.	(Margie's view vs. others' views) *Decision makers:* they know what skills are needed at the next level, and also what others say about Margie's ability to lead. *Margie:* she knows the long hours and extra work she has been putting in. Also, different implicit rules: Margie: she assumes that seniority matters—promotions are a reward for hard work, and you learn the new job on the job. *Her boss:* he believes you don't promote until the skills needed in the new job are evident.	(from Margie's point of view) What's right is that I have less experience with the budgeting process than other candidates. What's right is that if I understand the criteria for promotion, whether I agree with them or not, I can make an informed decision about my own goals and next steps.

This "right spotting" exercise is really good for difficult feedback sessions. It allows you to acknowledge the differences, and then inquire about what *is* accurate about the feedback. I coach one PM who is highly resistant to any feedback (it makes for amusing coaching sessions when the other person has their deflector shields up the entire time). This right spotting technique really helped in my work with this PM. I was able to acknowledge all the differences in our views, and still come back to the question, "What's right—or possibly right—about the feedback?" Again, the 2% rule: is anything useful?

The final concept I'll share from this excellent book is one called "stepping back." Specifically, they call it taking three steps back. Whenever feedback is given, it helps to consider it on three levels:

1. The relationship between the giver and receiver is the first step back. The giver and receiver each have personalities and these will interact in some way. The giver may be very direct and blunt, whereas the receiver may be sensitive and shy. So, taking one step back and recognizing the relationship between the two is important.
2. The roles in the firm are the second step back. Each person has a role in the firm and this affects how they interact to some degree. The chief compliance officer, the lead PM, the chief sales officer, and so on will each carry "baggage" because of their roles in the firm. Often, a second step back will help clarify the existence and nature of this baggage and allow the feedback message to be separated out and heard.
3. The third step back is a systems view (especially interesting). Employees in a firm operate in a system. How does the system affect feedback exchanges? If the culture of the firm is especially polite, then feedback may be watered down and ineffective. Perhaps employees have learned to use soft labels that don't really mean anything, such as "be more proactive." This allows the recipient to nod and say "okay" without having the faintest idea what the feedback really means!

Understanding that all feedback exchanges are affected at all three levels is important to remaining objective and "above the line." Of all the good tips in this book, this final one about three steps back will probably be the most helpful.

Please send me feedback on this appendix, so I can decide which trigger it activates in me and how I can best dismiss it without acknowledging any defensiveness.

---

[117] Douglas Stone and Sheila Heen, *Thanks for the Feedback* (Penguin, 2014), https://www.amazon. com/Thanks-Feedback-Science-Receiving-Well/dp/0143127136/ref=sr_1_1?s=books&ie=UT-F8&qid=1525901775&sr=1-1&keywords=thanks+for+the+feedback

Appendix F: Givers and Takers in the Investment World

Investment professionals live in a "takers" world. For every trade, there is a buyer and a seller, and one will win and the other will lose. This basic truth underlies the mindset of many investment pros. They look at life as a win/lose proposition. Smart people play to win. The largest component of most bonus plans is "individual contribution." Teamwork is given lots of lip service, but the real money is for the star. Second-tier players can take comfort in the warm glow of the team, but not in the extra pay that stars get!

One anecdotal bit of evidence from my twenty years of consulting is that only three leaders have offered to pay for a useful session that was considered simply a "coffee to reconnect." After these sessions, the leaders said, "Let me pay you for this time, it was very valuable." I suppose one explanation could be that I've only been useful in three sessions over twenty years, but my suspicion is that the "taker" mentality is at work: "Wonderful, I got all that information for free! I win!"

Another example is the CIO who complains that his CEO won't allocate funds for a second FCG offsite even though the first one was extremely productive. Hence, he can't schedule it. Really? We're talking about $9,000. That amount is a rounding error relative to a CIO's wealth. Why doesn't the CIO just pop for it himself? Again, the "taker" mentality cries, "Hey, I won't let this firm take advantage of me! If they aren't paying for it, I ain't doing it!" Penny wise and pound foolish. (Or, maybe the FCG offsite wasn't really that good, and this is the easiest way to let us down softly.)

The "taker" mindset shows up in the willingness to express appreciation (an emotional form of giving.) Investment firms are woefully short on giving appreciation. When investment leaders are asked why this is, three responses are typical:

1. Appreciation?! We PAY them, don't we?!
2. If we appreciate them, they will want more of #1.
3. And worse, if we appreciate them, they will become complacent and still want more of #1.

Really? All our experience with investment staffs indicate just the opposite! If you appreciate the staff, they will require less tangible pay (i.e., money) because they are receiving more intangible rewards (i.e., appreciation). And they will work harder. And be more loyal.

Enter Adam Grant and his Give/Take model.[118] Grant makes a wonderfully solid case for the benefits of being a giver. Citing many behavioral studies (like the "ultimatum game"), game theory ("prisoner's dilemma"), and examples from real life (Ken Lay as a taker, George Meyer [*The Simpsons*] as a giver), Grant makes a powerful case for being a generous leader whose guiding mantra is to "help people." Isn't that the purpose of our fiduciary profession? Aren't we supposed to be helping people plan for retirement? Shouldn't we *all* be givers, not takers? (In the sense that we are supposed to be putting the client's interests above all else: that is helping them.)

Here's the trick. The "giver" mentality must be genuine. It doesn't work if you fake it: I will give so that I can get more (ha, ha! I win again!)! Instead, it must come from a genuine sense of empathy: I give because it feels good to help others. Or, put slightly differently, I give because it is the decent thing to do. (Principled people may see it more as a rational action than a feeling.)

Grant's research reveals a set of core values for takers and givers, shown in Table F.1.

Table F.1 Taker/Giver Core Values

Taker Values	Giver Values
Wealth (money, material possessions)	Helpfulness (working for the well-being of others)
Power (dominance, control over others)	Responsibility (being dependable)
Pleasure (enjoying life)	Social justice (caring for the disadvantaged)
Winning (doing better than others)	Compassion (responding to the needs of others)

Note that the taker values are associated more with "self" and "ego," whereas the giver values are associated more with "selfless" and "other"-orientation. Maslow would place the taker values in the bottom three areas of his hierarchy, whereas the giver values are more representative of self-actualized people. There is nothing wrong with any of the listed values; they are common to all of us. Who doesn't want enough money or some occasional pleasures? However, in "the majority of the world's cultures [70 countries], including that of the United States, the majority of people endorse giving as their single most important guiding principle."[119]

So, why do so many professionals seem to endorse the "taker" side of the values chart? Grant writes, "The fear of being judged as weak or naïve prevents many people from acting like givers at work."[120] Grant explores the pressures that most of us feel in this tug of war between giving and taking:

> People who prefer to give often feel pressured to lean in the taker direction when they perceive the workplace as zero-sum. Whether it's a company with forced ranking systems, a group of companies vying to win the same clients, or a school with required grading curves and more demand than supply for desirable jobs, it's only natural to assume that peers will lean more towards taking than giving. "When they anticipate self-interested behavior from others," explains Stanford psychologist Dale Miller, "people feel that they'll be exploited if they operate like givers, so they conclude that 'pursuing a competitive orientation is the rational and appropriate thing to do.'" There's even evidence that just putting on a business suit and analyzing a Harvard Business School case study is enough to significantly reduce the attention that people pay to relationships and the interests of others. The fear of exploitation by takers is so pervasive, writes the Cornell economist Robert Frank, that "by encouraging us to expect the worst in others it brings out the worst in us: dreading the role of the chump, we are often loathe to heed our nobler instincts."[121]

FCG clients who have played out the Prisoner's Dilemma exercise with us will see a close correlation between takers/competitors (red behavior) and givers/collaborators (green behavior). Game theory teaches us the following lessons about takers (red) and givers (green):

1. In teams, lead with green behavior (win/win). It sends a signal: I want to collaborate. I want to build trust.
2. Reciprocate with green (W/W). This shows your desire to also collaborate and build trust.
3. Check out misunderstandings. When you play green (are a giver), and your colleague seems to play red (as a taker), then have the courage to inquire about the perceived disconnect. We have found that "Help me understand why you did such-and-such. That seemed like a red move (Win for him, lose for you)" works well as an inquiry.
4. Be willing to forgive, forget, and move on. We're all human, we all make mistakes.

And shame on the business schools: Teaching all of us that the reason why businesses exist is to "maximize shareholder wealth." This elevation of the profit motive goes against our basic desire to help others. Business schools should teach that a business exists to provide value to people. In return for providing value, a business makes a profit. The core of business should be about providing value by helping others. Even the brilliant Milton Friedman got sucked into believing that a business exists to make a profit. *Buyer beware*. From a giver perspective, a business exists to help people and in so doing, makes a profit.

My 40 years in the investment world support the preceding finding that many investment pros want to help others. They do have a generous mindset. But, as described in the quoted passage, they often suppress it because of the belief that it doesn't serve them to be givers in the investment world. I would love to see the mindset of our profession change to a giver mindset. Grant's fine book makes the intellectual case for how givers can end up on top of the success ladder. In fact, he shows that mindsets typically finish in this way:

1. Generous and wise people: on top ("Successful Givers")
2. Matchers: people who operate on a tit-for-tat basis
3. Takers (win/lose mentality): Get all that I can, can all that I get, and then poison the well!
4. Generous but naïve (Doormats): Givers who don't recognize the "wolf in sheep's clothing."
5. Apathetic: low concern for self and others ("Hey dude, whatever …")

Grant offers the chart in Table F.2.

Table F.2 Concern Grid

Concern for Self-Interest	Low	High
Low	Apathetic	**Selfless:** Self-sacrificing givers, "doormats"
High	**Selfish:** Takers/Matchers	**Otherish:** Successful Givers

For me, it was so heartening to read what I've always believed: that good people can finish first. Decent and kind people—providing they are also wise—can finish on top of the success ladder. This reminds me of the Biblical passage: *"be wise as serpents and harmless as doves."* (Matthew 10:16). This combination of compassion/kindness with wisdom is the mindset that provides the greatest level of success and happiness. Paraphrasing Albert Schweitzer: "I don't know what your calling will be, but I can tell you this. Whatever you do, you will only be happy if you find a life of service." Joy comes from contributing—and Grant's book makes this case compellingly.

So, be selfish and learn to give. You'll feel great *and* be more successful, paradoxical as it sounds.

---

[118] Adam M. Grant, *Give and Take* (Penguin, 2013), https://www.amazon.com/Give-Take-Helping-Others-Success-ebook/dp/B00AFPTSI0/ref=sr_1_1?s=books&ie=UTF8&qid=1525908093&s-r=1-1&keywords=give+and+take+adam+grant

[119] *Ibid.*, p. 21.

[120] *Ibid.*, p. 22.

[121] *Ibid.*, p. 43.

Appendix G: Complexity Thinking: Managing Polarities

Earlier in this book we praised teamwork and underlined its importance to success. But guess what? Teamwork is *not* the answer.

"What!" Shocked response from paying clients. "We hired you to improve our teamwork! Where was the discussion about 'not the answer' during the sales pitch for team development!?"

Deep breath. Relax. Teamwork *is* important to success, now more than ever. But teamwork must not be thought of in a simplistic fashion. As with most aspects of life, teamwork has an upside and a downside. Each must be considered as a firm aims to improve performance. This exercise requires complexity thinking: Both/and vs. Either/or.

Let's follow the path of teamwork in the following charts, inspired by Barry Johnson's work on polarities.[122] Firm leaders come to FCG asking for guidance in building strong teams. We are happy to help. We have wonderful diagnostics to determine what aspects of teamwork require attention. Typically, the presenting problem is described as in Figure G.1.

Figure G.1 Teamwork Problems

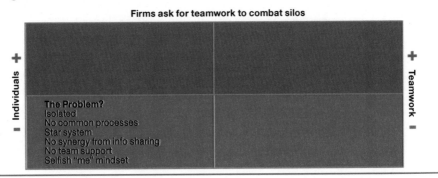

The staff members are mostly acting as individual contributors. They are producing good work, but missing all the opportunities offered by teamwork: sharing information, learning from one another, establishing common processes, building a strong culture, and so on. In brief, they operate in an isolated way, sometimes resembling a star system, in which the competitive juices are turned inward and morale suffers. Understandably, leaders recognize the limitations of this arrangement and decide that something must be done. So, "who ya gonna call?" (cue the theme from *Ghostbusters*): FCG gets a call to change the focus from individual to team.

FCG has had success moving a team to the upper right quadrant, where the positive aspects of team are operating, shown in Figure G.2.

Figure G.2 Teamwork Solutions

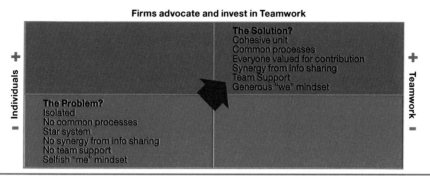

If FCG has done its job right, the result is a more cohesive unit, with common processes. Instead of promoting stars, leaders promote teamwork by emphasizing the important role that each person plays. Further, there are benefits from synergy—sharing information and processes—and from aiding co-workers when necessary (e.g., family issues, medical emergencies, and so on). The selfish "me" mindset becomes more of a "we" mindset. So, all good, right? Well, yes. This phase of teaming is good, and teams that achieve it benefit. Productivity and morale improve.

However (there is always a "but," right?), almost inevitably this wonderful state of teaming turns south at some point and shows its negative side. The downside of teaming is shown in Figure G.3.

Figure G.3 Teaming Downsides

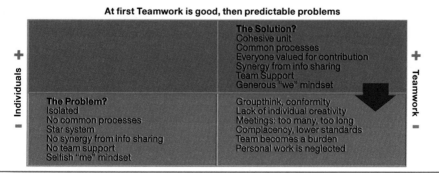

Often FCG is called in to address these problems, which are the opposite of too much individual focus: *too much* focus on teamwork. Teams can become complacent and stifling, canceling out individual initiative and creativity. Efforts to create team spirit become tedious: mandatory bowling parties, scavenger hunts, and the like. The emphasis on teamwork sucks time away from important think time. Knowledge workers need uninterrupted periods of concentration, but the ethos of a team says, "Isolating yourself is bad. You must spend time collaborating with the team. Manage by walking around." This team emphasis can limit creative and productive work.

Eventually a "crusader" (someone who recognizes the need for change) will push for more individual and less team. This push for individualism will often be met by a defender of the merits of teamwork. The argument from the defender is, "Team is great, we just need to return to being a *good* team" (i.e., move back above the line). But then the crusaders will argue that neither form of team allows for enough individuality: what's needed is a return to the benefits of participating as an individual. So, the dynamic of the four-square changes once again, this time to the upper left: strong individual performance, which looks like Figure G.4.

Figure G.4 Individual Performance Strengths

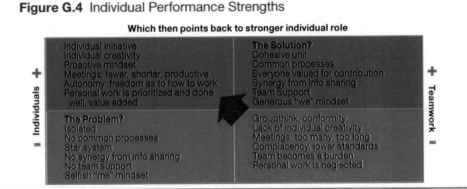

Hence, we've come full circle, from the individual mindset being the major problem to the individual mindset being the solution. The difference, of course, is realizing the positive side of the individual, not the negative. When individuals are untethered, amazing things can happen: More creativity, more initiative, more value-add. Typically, individual orientations allow for more time to do the work and less time taken up by meetings of questionable value. Engagement is high and productivity is strong.

So, is the upper left box the answer? No. The point of polarity management is that there is no final resting point, no final solution. In this dynamic situation—individual vs. teamwork—leaders will have to continually manage the balance. The goal is to spend as much time above the line—in the positive zones—as possible. The dynamic movement will represent an infinity loop, as shown in Figure G.5.

Figure G.5 The Dynamic Infinity Loop

Notice the placement of the infinity symbol, slightly above the middle line. That placement represents ideal management of this polarity system. Watch the dynamic circle around from one quadrant to another, all the time working to manage it back above the line in the positive quadrants.

In the investment world, there are numerous examples of polarities, which have to be continuously managed rather than "solved" (i.e., dealt with once and for all). This task requires complexity thinking—embracing both/and—rather than simplistic thinking— one or the other. Table G.1 a shows some common polarities that FCG has encountered. In each case, there is a positive and negative for each pole.

Table G.1 Polarities

Growth of assets ("sales-centric")	Performance of funds ("investment-centric")
Short term	Long term
Centralized decision making	Decentralized
Owner interests	Client interests
Individual rewards	Group rewards
Creativity	Structure
Decisiveness	Flexibility
Direct, blunt communication	Tactful, polite communication

So, how does one manage polarities effectively? Johnson recommends these five steps:

1. An awareness of the difference between a solvable problem and a polarity to be managed.
2. An awareness that there is an upside and a downside to each pole.
3. Sensitivity to the downsides as they are experienced.
4. A willingness to move from the downside of one pole to the upside of the other, knowing that the process will return to the present pole in the future. (The quadrants cycle over time, creating an infinity loop.)
5. An understanding of the two dynamic forces involved in all the dilemmas (**Crusading** for the new quadrant vs. **Defending** the merits of the status quo). This includes an ability to be effective in Crusading, Defending, and mediating between the two.

For any polarity that leaders are wrestling with—like the one discussed in this appendix concerning individuals and teamwork—it's useful to create the four-square and spell out the pros and cons of each. Identify which quadrant you are currently in. Then devise a strategy to remain above the line, knowing that you will dip below it periodically. When viewed this way, leaders move from simplistic "either/or" solutions to a more sophisticated "both/and" approach—that is, complexity thinking.

That's why teamwork is not *the* answer. It's part of a system that has to be managed.

---

122 Barry Johnson, *Polarity Management: Identifying and Managing Unsolvable Problems* (HRD Press, 2014).

Appendix H: Debates: Making Them Open and Productive

Open and productive debates win out. They allow teams to make the best decisions, and good decisions characterize the best firms. Most firms don't do this well. Read on and learn how to do better.

Framing the discussion is crucial. In other words, before jumping into the topic—no matter how juicy—get the playing field marked off and the rules clearly defined. The model shown in Figure H.1 has been tried and tested over decades. It works. Its elements are explained in this appendix.

Figure H.1 Elements of Framing

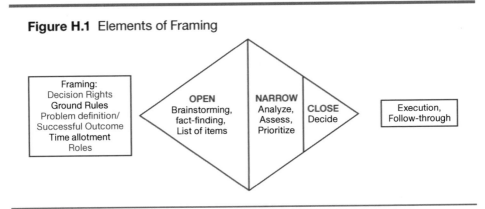

Let's take the elements in order.

Decision Rights

Before you even start a discussion, decide HOW the decision will be made. Establish who has the final authority over decisions. That person then has the right to decide how a decision will be made from the diagram in Figure H.2. The flow of the chart is from command-and-control (deciding alone and telling them) to consensus (everyone favors the decision).

Figure H.2 Decision Flow Chart

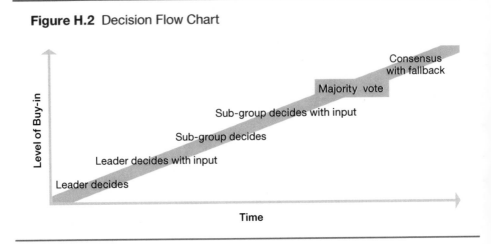

For example, the person with decision rights might say, "We'll discuss/debate this idea for 30 minutes, then after getting that input, I'll make the decision." Or she could say, "We'll discuss for 30 minutes, then vote." The point is to make it very clear how the decision will be reached. This helps people address their arguments toward the neutral decision maker and not "at" the other debater(s). This works like in a courtroom, where the lawyers address the jury or the judge but not the other lawyer. Without a jury or judge, the two debaters start to go after each other, and safety is lost.

Ground Rules

When decision rights have been made clear, set out ground rules. The goal of ground rules is to *create safety*. Good conversations take place only when team members feel safe to express themselves openly and honestly. Leaders play a big part in creating safety. A major derailer of safety is retribution. If people have been "punished" for speaking their minds, then the precedent is set clearly: don't be candid … or else. Don't oppose the boss's view. Two very useful ground rules are:

1. **Mutual Purpose:** The beneficial outcome of the conversation should be very clear. For example, a highest-level goal could be "create a vision of success." Presumably, everyone will agree on the importance of this goal. As we'll cover later, however, the actual discussion should be narrowed down from this very broad topic.
2. **Mutual Respect:** Although all team members will typically pay lip service to this behavior, many quickly toss it aside once the debate starts. A useful way to think about preserving respect is to "stay on your side of the table." If you imagine a table and you are sitting across from the other debater, stay on your side. Your side represents your reality, your views, your "space." Any statement about the other person or his views is considered reaching across the table. An example: "That idea is wrong. It doesn't make sense." This language can be inflammatory, which is what you are trying to avoid. You have to stay away from the playground dialogue of "did so," "did not," "did so," "did not." You could make the same point by saying: "I don't see it that way. I don't understand your point." The difference is subtle but important. The first way invites a reactive response, because it's inflammatory. The second simply states your reality, without attacking the other person's. It shows respect.

The term we use at FCG for noninflammatory language is *forthright diplomacy*. This language is candid but tactful. Good debaters use both candor and curiosity.

Problem Definition/Successful Outcome

Using the preceding example, "create a vision of success" has to be narrowed. Too many conversations we've witnessed eventually derail because the topic is too broad. Participants go off in different directions. Let's use a real example involving "vision of success." Participants should have a well-articulated goal and process. When FCG works with the vision question, we frame it by asking participants to think in terms of stakeholders: What does each of them want? What does success look like for Clients, Employees, and Owners? (We call this our "CEO" approach to vision.) To narrow and focus the conversation, we do one at a time. We may start with "What does success look like for your clients?" That framing usually creates an animated and focused conversation.

Time Allotment

As indicated earlier, another good guideline—or boundary—is to make a clear statement about time. If people are long-winded or tend to filibuster, then use a smartphone to keep time for speaking (say, three minutes to make your case). You can assign a specific person to be the "time cop."

Roles

Another way to help debates stay on track is to have clearly assigned roles. The person with decision rights acts like the "judge" in the courtroom. He remains neutral as the debate rolls on, and brings down the gavel when someone is out of order (using inflammatory language). Other roles that are sometimes assigned are: timekeeper (mentioned above), devil's advocate (purposely stating the other side of the argument), subject-matter expert (someone who presents "expert testimony" about the given topic). These typical roles are shown in Figure H.3.

Figure H.3 Typical Roles

| Time Cop | Decision Maker | Devil's Advocate | Subject Expert |

These framing elements produce a better debate. Once established, the Open-Narrow-Close (ONC) model offers a proven way to move through the decision-making process. Using the "Vision" example, here's how the ONC model works.

OPEN: This phase of the model is the creative "right-brain" process of getting ideas on the table. Typical brainstorming rules apply: no criticism, go for quantity (not quality), challenge assumptions. In the CEO model, working with the "C" (Clients), the question might be, "What does success look like concerning clients?" A list might include:

- Retention rates
- Satisfaction levels
- Investment performance
- Client service
- Consistency
- (etc.)

NARROW: The second phase, Narrow, brings in the "left brain," which begins to analyze and categorize the data. Many investment professionals are especially good at this process. The problem is that they start doing their thing while still in the OPEN phase. We call this mistake *premature evaluation* and we liken it to driving on both sides of the road (American vs. British rules of the road). If you allow motorists to drive on both sides simultaneously, a mess will ensue. Same with discussions. The leader (judge) must watch for this derailer and bang the gavel when it occurs. In this narrowing phase, the real debate takes place. It is appropriate here for both sides on a given topic to present their best thinking, and to provide point-counterpoint. The key is to be able to do this in the spirit of safety and respect. Two particularly powerful phrases that help are: "I see it differently …" (vs. "You're wrong") and "Help me understand …" (vs. "You're not making sense").

Note: Safety does *not* imply soft or superficial debates. Quite the contrary: "Hard on the ideas, easy on the people" is the mantra. When FCG facilitates a debate, we encourage probing, prodding, and provocative questions, but those can be asked in a respectful way. Safety also implies no retribution: I'm not punished for asking a hard question, and I'm not humiliated for responding, "I don't know"(as long as it's followed up by "But I'll find out").

CLOSE: After ideas have been properly vetted in the time frame allotted, the decision rights holder (or time cop) recognizes that the time for debate is up and moves toward a decision based on the already-determined method.

A good debate should end with a decision and action step. This involves clarity on: Who will do What by When. Too many good decisions are watered down or lost completely due to sloppy execution. (This is a longer topic for another day.)

This process for open and productive debate works. However, it requires conscious, conscientious leadership and proactive participation. Leaders must do the work of good leaders—establish rules and order—and they must pay attention to the tone of the debate. If it becomes personal and disrespectful, then intervene. For example, suggest that the conversation has dropped under the line (without blaming anyone) and that a five-minute break would be helpful. Participants are responsible for understanding and following the process: most importantly, by practicing respect and avoiding inflammatory language. Always remember: the key to successful debates is safety. When that is lost, the group's only goal is to get it back. Nothing productive happens when people are defensive. Safety sounds so simple, but it is very hard to achieve in practice. We all have our insecurities and they are easily triggered. Welcome to the delicate art of open and productive debate! Like anything worthwhile, it takes time and attention to do it well.

Appendix I: Client-Centric Culture–Reality or Blindspot?

Which is more important to you: time with family or time at work? We all know the predictable answer: family. Yet many pros' schedules would suggest that work usually trumps family, with many more hours spent at the office or on the road than at home. (This essay was written on Thanksgiving Day: can you say, "Guilty as charged!")

Similarly, we all know the "correct" answer to the following question: Which stakeholder is top priority at your firm? The client, right? The kind people at the Portfolio Management Association of Canada (PMAC) invited me to speak at their annual meeting of investment leaders and allowed me to collect some data on this topic. Table I.1 shows the vote in the room of about 100 investment leaders.

Table I.1 Stakeholder Priority

Which stakeholder is top priority at your firm?	
Clients	76
Owners	19
Employees	9

Indeed, if we review the hundreds of culture surveys FCG has done for asset management firms, the top value chosen is "client satisfaction":

1. Client Satisfaction—44%[123]
2. Professional—42%
3. Ethical/Integrity—38%
4. Collaboration/Teamwork—37%

Many CEOs are shocked when they see that their firm's client satisfaction number is less than 100%! They gasp, "How can any of our staff not vote for Client Satisfaction? Why isn't the number 100%?" An appropriate response and a fair question. Some staff members have told us privately, "Client Satisfaction is a given, so I didn't want to 'waste' one of my votes on it." Nevertheless, the survey results are out of kilter with the polling results from PMAC, where the audience response was well over 70%.

So, if we dig into this question of client-centricity, what do we find? As you might expect, we find a range of answers. Many firms we survey appear to be very client-centric, especially the firms we call "Focus Elite."[124] These firms also don't reach 100% for client satisfaction, but they are significantly higher than the average firm (Table I.2).

Table I.2 Client Satisfaction Vote Reults

	Client Satisfaction
Focus Elite Firms	56%
Investment Industry	44%

FCG knows these firms well and can say with confidence that they do place clients ahead of all other stakeholders. For example, Table I.3 is another culture survey chart which asks, "What are the leaders most focused on: gathering assets or investment performance?" The more typical firm is on the left, the Focus Elite firm on the right.

Table I.3 Leaders' Focus: Asset gathering vs. investment performance

	Focus Elite Firm A	Focus Elite Firm B
Leaders are mostly focused on asset gathering (sales-centic)	37%	0%
Neutral	42%	11%
Leaders are mostly focused on fund performance (investment-centric)	21%	89%

The firm on the left has many staff members who believe that leadership is mostly concerned with growing AUM. In sharp contrast, the Focus Elite firm on the right has no such staff members. The Focus Elite message is clear: first and foremost, we want to perform for our clients. (Note: FCG is not anti-growth! Our view is that growth is fine as long as clients remain the top priority.)

Further review of culture surveys for many firms revealed some truly alarming results. The firm XYZ, whose results are shown in Table I.4, had not chosen "client satisfaction" in either the current or aspirational culture. (We will pause here to give you a moment to gasp …)

Table I.4 Aspirational Culture

Which values/behaviors best describe your preferred culture, that is, the one that would best allow the firm to realize its vision of success?			
	# of Responses	XYZ%	Industry%
Excellence/Continuous Improvement	29	51%	41%
Professional	23	40%	33%
Respect	23	40%	23%
Passion/Energy/Motivate	23	40%	21%
Ethical/Integrity	21	37%	39%
Long Term Perspective/Vision	20	35%	43%
Competitive/Win/Be the Best	20	35%	15%
Collaboration/Teamwork	19	33%	41%
Intelligent	19	33%	26%
Entrepreneurial Meritocracy tied	18	32%	21%

N = 57

Can you imagine the CEO of this firm sharing these results with clients? That would be a "Madoff moment." No doubt this firm's staff did choose some fine values—excellence, professional, integrity, collaboration, etc.—but the client would still be left wondering, "Where the heck are WE in the voting?"

Even more intriguing is the result from the sales team at a different investment firm (Table I.5). This is the group of people who are specifically called on to take good care of clients!

Table I.5 Sales Team Values

Top 10 values for the same sales group, aspirational!		
	# of Responses	**ABC%**
Accountability/Responsibility	9	43%
Commitment	9	43%
Professional	9	43%
Ethical/Integrity	8	38%
Collaboration/Teamwork	8	38%
Excellence/Continuous Improvement	7	33%
Results Oriented	7	33%
Candor/Honesty/Open	7	33%
Clear Performance Goals	6	29%
Expense Control	6	29%

N = 21

How is it possible that the sales and client-facing people are not choosing "client satisfaction" in their aspirational view of the firm? (Interlude for head scratching …)

In part, the explanation may come from survey responses aimed at explaining what is most meaningful to staff members at investment firms. The results of six firms are shown in Table I.6, and they are very typical of what we see in the industry.

Table I.6 Motivation Results

Motivation: What has the most meaning in daily experience? (choose 2)	
The work serves a larger purpose, doing something positive in the world (such as allocating capital property in the markets.)	8%
The work contributes to a sound and sustainable financial future for our firm.	15%
The work benefits our clients, and I enjoy happy clients most of all about my job.	23%
The work allows me to spend time with bright and engaging collegues. I like these team interactions best of all.	22%
The work is interesting, challenging and intellectually stimulating.	32%

N = 968, froms 6 forms. 3 US, 2 European, 1 Canadian

Most investment professionals are motivated by the nature of the work. They love the challenge and intellectual stimulation of solving problems. After that choice, their motivation is split equally between clients and colleagues. Please note: FCG is not proposing a conspiracy theory that investment firms are actively working *against* their clients! Not at all. But like the professional who says, "My family is most important," the industry pros seem largely unaware of the disconnect between what they say and what they do; there's a "say-do" gap. Would it be useful to be more aware of the disconnect and then make adjustments, rather than leave it untouched as a blindspot? On this point specifically, one of the PMAC votes showed a lot of honesty and self-awareness. FCG asked them the question shown in Table I.7, which also shows the answers.

Table I.7 Client Orientation Results

Moment of Truth: At our firm, there have been some times when clients did not come first.	
Agree	67%
Neutral	1%
Disagree	32%

Two-thirds of those in the room responded that, indeed, sometimes the client does not come first. If the first step in solving a problem is to acknowledge it, then this could be a healthy first step: awareness. FCG has certainly witnessed many strategy sessions in which the profitability of the firm came first. Clients were not treated with disrespect—as in the now-famous Goldman Sachs example in which clients were deemed "muppets"—but nevertheless firm profitability was paramount.

FCG brainstormed examples from our client experience of "client first" vs. "profit first" and came up with the examples in Table I.8.

Table I.8 Mindset Difference Examples

Client centric:	Profit mindset:
1. Performance	1. Asset gathering
2. Closing funds	2. Keeping funds open
3. Fees alogned with performance (fair)	3. Fees indifferent to performance (max)
4. Solution orented, refer clients to best solution (custom)	4. Sell hot products, create funds to take it all (scale)
5. Investment process and teams are top notch	5. Investment engine is broken, but still promoted to clients

Discussing them in order:

1. Are the leaders focused on delivering results to the clients, first and foremost, or do they lean toward gathering assets? An example of this occurred in a firm in which the CEO was very sales-minded and was always looking for opportunities to grow. His CIO told him, "We should close our flagship fund. It has reached capacity." The CIO thought they had reached an agreement: no more new assets. Within a week, the CEO met with a prospect who wanted to add $200 million to the flagship fund. At first the CEO held the line and said, "No." Then the moment of truth arrived. The prospect said, "Okay, how about $400 million?" The CEO's response: "Done!" Later that year, the CIO left the firm, citing that incident as the "straw that broke the camel's back."

2. A different firm had grown its flagship fund to a sizable level. FCG asked the CIO of the firm, "What is the optimal size of this fund?" The response: "About half of its current level." Again, if the client is really the top priority, then this fund should have been closed long before.

3. The fee question is increasingly relevant. FCG has written elsewhere about Baillee Gifford in Scotland whose partners have lowered fees for various products simply because they thought it was the right thing to do. Contrast that decision with a CEO in London who asked his lead salesman to continue charging 100 basis points for a product that was getting roughly half that fee in the market. The sales person—clearly of high integrity—quit, stating, "I don't want my legacy to be: 'he over-charged the clients for as long as he could.'"

4. The idea here is that if you really place the client first, you will look for best solutions—even if that means referring the client elsewhere. One of FCG's Focus Elite firms has done this, so don't shake your head and say, "Well, in the real world *that* would never happen." It does. In that case it happened because the firm in question really believes that the only way to build absolute trust with clients is to always give them the best deal. The opposite extreme is to promote "hot dot" products that inevitably will collapse, hurting the client and leading to the wonderful graphic by Carl Richards (Figure I.1).

Figure I.1

BehaviorGap.com

5. The firms with high integrity and client-first mindset work tirelessly to keep their investment teams and process in top shape. Therefore, they can promote the products in good conscience. Conversely, FCG has worked with investment teams whose process is broken—by their own admission—but is still being actively marketed by the firm to consultants and clients. Can these firms honestly say, "Clients come first?"

After discussing these two different mindsets with the PMAC audience, I then asked them to vote on which behaviors/attitudes would best help to build a client-centric culture. The result (Table I.9) is instructive.

Table I.9 Behaviors for a Client-Centric Culture

Which behaviors/attitudes below would best help to build a client-centric culture? (Trust/ethics is a given) (3 votes)	
More listening	25%
More accountability	19%
More excellence/continued improvement	15%
More candor	10%
More empathy	10%
More curiosity	5%
More respect	5%
More caring	4%
More discipline	4%
More clarity and precision	3%

The audience selected "more listening" by a wide margin. FCG interprets this vote as a clear indication that tuning in to the needs of the client is the real key to client-centric cultures. Another word for tuning in to another's needs is *empathy*, which also got a significant number of votes. In our view, empathy/listening would be core to a truly client-first firm. A recent *Harvard Business Review* article, entitled "Empathy Is Still Lacking in the Leaders Who Need It Most,"[125] stated:

> Frankly, when empathy kept coming up in our research, I was surprised.
> All of the people we interviewed were serious business executives.
> Empathy was not the first virtue I associated with the rough and tumble
> of today's highly competitive business world. I expected to hear about
> boldness, perseverance, and toughness. Later, when we reported the
> results of our research to other leaders, many said empathy was the most
> important of the five attributes we had uncovered. Why? Because empathy

enables those who possess it to see the world through others' eyes and understand their unique perspectives.

These authors concludes that "[t]oday's multiple and highly vocal audiences demand to be heard or they will take their business elsewhere. You need empathy to know who those audiences are and what they want."

This final statement nicely combines empathy with listening (i.e., "demand to be heard"). To be a client-centric culture in today's world, you need pros who listen to and empathize with clients. Then, they must have the courage to do the right thing: *put the client first.*

In addition to empathy, FCG has identified several other characteristics of client-first investment firms, as shown below in Table I.10.

Table I.10 Client-First Firm Characteristics

Client First Mindset	Profit First Mindset
Profession	Business
Serve	Compete
Win/win	Win/lose
Client trusts you	Buyer Beware

The mindsets on the right are not "bad" mindsets. For example, you would want your traders to have these mindsets. When they are trading positions in the markets, they must compete and win. That is appropriate. The problem occurs when these mindsets become the mainstay of the entire organization, including the client-facing professionals! Serving through good listening and empathy must be foremost in the client-first firm.

Returning to our original point about blindspots, FCG maintains that many investment firms have a blindspot around client-centrism. These firms are run by good people with good intentions—no question. But, like the professionals who say, "My top priority is my family" and then spend nearly all their time working, there is a disconnect between what they say and what they do. There is a values clash. The professional wants to succeed at work—which requires time and effort—but she or he also wants to be a good spouse and parent. Balance is required ... and often some tough choices. Likewise, the investment firm that wants to be client-centric must find the balance between serving its various stakeholders. The first step in finding the right balance is to recognize the blindspot: that we are often placing commercial success (i.e., profit) ahead of client interests.

So, what's to be done? FCG recommends that investment leaders eliminate the blindspot by making client-first a regular topic at meetings and strategy sessions. Encourage staff members to filter every decision through the "client-first" value. Also encourage all team members to practice empathy: How will the client view this decision? Illuminating the blindspot will not eliminate all tough choices, but it will bring integrity to the process. It will make for a clear-eyed view of all the options.

(Upon completing this essay, I did join my family for our Thanksgiving celebration ...)

---

[123] Percent of respondents who chose this as a value in their firm's culture. Averaged over all the surveys (hundreds) FCG has done.

[124] The FCG Focus Elite firms are described in our paper titled "Linking Strong Culture to Success." See our website for a copy of this white paper: http://www.focuscgroup.com/wp-content/uploads/2015/11/Linking_Strong_Culture_to_Success.pdf

[125] Ernest Wilson III, "Empathy Is Still Lacking in the Leaders Who Need It Most," *Harvard Business Review* (September 21, 2015).

About the Author

 **James Ware, CFA,** founded the Focus Consulting Group in 1999. He has authored three prior books on investing, and numerous articles appearing in *The Financial Analysts Journal, The Journal of Portfolio Management, Harvard Business Review, and CFA Magazine.* He is a frequent speaker at industry events, such as the CFA Annual, the Greenwich Roundtable, the U.S. Delegates CIO Roundtable, and the Financial Analysts Seminar. His academic background is Williams College and the University of Chicago Business School. He lives with his wife and two daughters in Long Grove, Illinois.

Focus Consulting Group Services

Serving over 400 clients in 20 countries for nearly 2 decades

OUR MISSION
To help investment leaders succeed by leveraging talent.

OUR APPROACH
We partner with investment firms to improve their effectiveness and their ability to add value to stakeholders.

LEADERSHIP: Increasing leadership effectiveness among self, team, firm

- 360 assessments for strengths, weaknesses, blind spots and development
- Executive coaching and change management
- Team analysis and diagnostics

CULTURE: Building a high performing, learning culture

- Culture analysis, diagnostics and debrief
- Culture management and industry comparison
- Benchmarking to attract and retain talent, improve decision-making

REWARDS AND INCENTIVES: Designing plans that are fair, transparent, and simple

- Industry benchmarks research
- Interviews and discovery of current and preferred reward philosophy
- Design and facilitation of total compensation and incentive plans

INVESTMENT PHILOSOPHY AND PROCESS: Defining and sharpening your team's decision making

- Philosophy and process, and talent assessments
- Leveraging behavioral finance tools and techniques
- Embedding with teams to observe and improve their process and execution

STRATEGY: Moving your firm to its preferred future

- SWOT analysis based on industry expertise

- Discussion and agreement on strategic planning process
- Connecting the strategic plan to responsibilities and your rewards system

SUCCESSION: Putting the right people in the right roles at the right time using a merit-based process

- Developing a talent pipeline
- Assessment of talent and facilitation of talent review
- Process for design and implementation of succession plan

TALENT MANAGEMENT: Managing the three C's approach: competence, contribution, criticality

- Understanding your firm's bench strength
- Managing performance through improved performance reviews and feedback
- Creating development paths for increasing skills, capabilities and performance: learning skills of high-performing investment teams

OFFSITE DESIGN AND FACILITATION: Getting the most from bringing the whole team/firm together

- C-suite or team dynamics, improving the performance through clear goal alignment
- Leadership development via "learning experiences" on various topics, such as better communication and mindfulness
- Increasing team effectiveness and development

COMMUNICATIONS: Boosting the impact of messaging for leaders, teams and client-facing professionals

- Improving team productivity, engagement and effectiveness through communications assessments and development programs
- Leveraging individual style through customized presentation coaching
- Strengthening client and prospect relationships by focusing on clarity, consistency and character in all forms of communication (verbal, written, non-verbal)

For more information about FCG's services, please contact:
Liz Severyns at lseveryns@focuscgroup.com

Mission
(WHY do we exist?)
Purpose statement

Vision of Success
(WHERE are we going?)
Goals and Metrics for stakeholders:
Clients | Employees | Owners

Culture
(WHO are we?)

☐ Has your firm indentified and aligned around a defined core set of values?

☐ Does your culture support the firm's mission and vision?

☐ Does your culture align with your strategy?

Strategy
(HOW do we get there?)

☐ Have you defined and communicated a strategic plan?

☐ How well does your strategic plan keep pace with the changes in the industry?

☐ How well does your staff understand the strategic plan and their role(s) in executing it?

☐ Do you review/update your strategic plan on an annual basis?

Do all of the following align with your firm's culture and strategy?

Leadership styles	**Rewards**
Talent	**Succession**
Investment Philosophy/Process	**Marketing/Sales/Client facing**

★ Assessments designed for measuring and tracking each

FOCUS CONSULTING GROUP

WWW.FOCUSCGROUP.COM

Index

98083346R00124

Made in the USA
Lexington, KY
04 September 2018